Neutrality After 1989

New Paths in the Post-Cold War World

EDITED BY NAMAN KARL-THOMAS HABTOM

E-INTERNATIONAL
RELATIONS
PUBLISHING

E-International Relations
Bristol, England
2024

ISBN: 978-1-910814-70-3

Production: Michael Tang
Cover Image: hpphtns/Shutterstock

A catalogue record for this book is available from the British Library.

E-International Relations

Editor-in-Chief and Publisher: Stephen McGlinchey
Books Editor: Bill Kakenmaster

Editorial assistance: Adeleke Olumide Ogunnoiki, Bhargavi PBA, Julian Izzo, Tara Yarwais, Vaishnav Rajkumar.

E-International Relations is the world's leading International Relations website and publisher. Our daily publications feature expert articles, reviews, podcasts and interviews – as well as student learning resources. The website is run by a non-profit organisation based in Bristol, England and staffed by an all-volunteer team. In addition to our website content, E-International Relations publishes a range of books.

As E-International Relations is committed to open access in the fullest sense, free versions of our books are available on our website https://www.e-ir.info/

Abstract

Following the collapse of the Soviet Union and the emergence of the United States as the world's sole superpower, neutrality was seen by many as a relic of the Cold War. However, the arrival of rising powers on the scene and the gradual shift towards multipolarity as countries like Russia and China assert their influence and challenge the US-dominated international order has in turn revived neutrality in its various forms. This book begins with a range of chapters examining the 'old neutrals' of Europe via contemporary Austrian and Swiss neutrality, the decline and end of Swedish and Finnish neutrality, and the resilience of Irish neutrality. Later chapters deal with the emergence of 'new neutrals' via examinations of Vietnamese 'bamboo diplomacy,' Israel's efforts to balance its relations with Washington and Moscow, and Oman's non-interventionist foreign policy. As the range of chapters show, the role of neutrality – and its perception or misperceptions – remain vital in understanding contemporary geopolitics and international relations.

About the Editor

Naman Karl-Thomas Habtom is a doctoral student at the Faculty of History, University of Cambridge. Previously, he has been a visiting researcher at the Swedish Defence University, Université libre de Bruxelles, and Stockholm University's Hans Blix Centre. His research focuses on contemporary European military and diplomatic history with a special focus on Sweden. His research interests also include neutrality, foreign fighters, and nuclear weapons policy. He has published articles in *Scandinavian Journal of History* and the *Scandinavian Journal of Military Studies* and has written on international affairs and security policy for *War on the Rocks*, *Lawfare,* and *Responsible Statecraft* among others.

Contributors

Roby C. Barrett is a Middle East and North Africa Forum Fellow and a scholar and Gulf expert with the Middle East Institute, Washington, DC. He is a former Foreign Service Officer with a background in intelligence and special operations. He has been a Senior Fellow and Instructor of Applied Intelligence at US Special Operations Command and a briefer and subject matter expert with Special Operations – US Central Command. He provides support to various US government organisations including the Office of the Secretary of Defense, the National Defense University, the State Department, and the intelligence community. He was a visiting professor at the Royal Saudi Arabian Command and Staff School focused on Gulf security (specifically Yemen and Iran), and a featured expert on Iran at the German Council on Foreign Relations and with the Bundeswehr. He holds a Ph.D. in Middle Eastern and South Asian History from the University of Texas at Austin.

Karen Devine is a former Chevening, Government of Ireland and Fulbright Scholar. She has authored a number of journal articles on Irish neutrality, and more broadly, the foreign, security, and defence policies of small states within the European Union. Her research interests include the influence of gender dynamics, public opinion and NGOs in international relations and she combines quantitative and poststructuralist approaches to understanding values and national identity as dynamics in public attitudes to foreign policy and the use of force. She teaches Irish Foreign Policy, European Union politics and policy, Gender and Politics and research methods at Dublin City University. She has published articles in peer-reviewed journals such as *International Political Science Review, Cooperation and Conflict, Swiss Political Science Review, New Zealand International Review, Irish Political Studies, Irish Studies in International Affairs*, and writes articles for numerous non-governmental organisation publications focusing on European Union politics and Irish neutrality.

Pascal Lottaz is an Associate Professor at Kyoto University where he investigates neutrality in international relations and directs the research network neutralitystudies.com. He received his MA and PhD from the National Graduate Institute for Policy Studies (GRIPS) and previously worked at Waseda University and Temple University (Japan Campus). His recent books include *Sweden, Japan, and the Long Second World War* (Routledge, 2022), *Neutral Beyond the Cold: Neutral States and the Post-Cold War International System* (Lexington Books, 2022), and *Notions of Neutralities* (Lexington Books, 2019). He also wrote entries on 'Neutrality Studies' for Oxford Encyclopedia and 'The Politics and Diplomacy of Neutrality' for Oxford Bibliography.

Nguyen Khac Giang is a Visiting Fellow at the Vietnam Studies Programme, ISEAS – Yusof Ishak Institute. He was formerly Head of the Political Research Unit of the Hanoi-based Vietnam Institute for Economic and Policy Research (VEPR). His academic work has appeared in, among others, *Asian Journal of Political Science*, *Contemporary Southeast Asia*, *Constitutional Political Economy*, *New Zealand Journal of Asian Studies* and *Asia & the Pacific Policy Studies*. He holds a PhD in Political Science from Victoria University of Wellington, New Zealand. He is a frequent commentator on Vietnamese affairs and writes extensively for Vietnamese and English news outlets.

Erik Noreen is Associate Professor of Peace and Conflict Studies at Uppsala University. His research is centred around international security, military intervention, Swedish foreign and security policy, threat images and socialisation, and the security of the Baltic Sea states. He has published on these topics in journals such as *European Journal of International Security*, *International Relations*, and *Journal of Peace Research*, and in volumes published by *Routledge*, *Ashgate*, and the *Johns Hopkins University Press*.

Jussi Pakkasvirta is a historian and professor of Area and Cultural Studies at the University of Helsinki. He has a long experience in research of Latin American history, culture and politics, and theories of nationalism. Pakkasvirta was the President of CEISAL, the European Council for Social Research on Latin America, from 2016 to 2019. His latest research projects have analyzed Finnish-Russian relations and Nordic-Spanish relations during the Cold War. He has written and edited fourteen monographs and published in journals such as *Nations and Nationalism, Cooperation and Conflict* and *Nordic Journal of Latin American and Caribbean Studies*. His other research interests are interdisciplinary methodologies, environmental conflicts, and the culture of social media.

Liudmila Samarskaia is a Research Fellow at the Center for Middle East Studies, Primakov National Research Institute of World Economy and International Relations, Russian Academy of Sciences (IMEMO RAS). Her research interests include the internal political development of Israel, its positions in the Middle Eastern regional arena and the history of Mandatory Palestine. She also taught Contemporary History of the Middle East at Moscow State University (MSU). Apart from articles in peer-reviewed journals and various online resources, she has authored several book chapters, the most recent being on Israeli politics in the Eastern Mediterranean.

Roxanna Sjöstedt is Associate Professor of Political Science at Lund University. Her research is centred around international security, military intervention, securitization, non-military threats, in particular epidemics, and the socialisation of minority rights norms. She has published on these topics in outlets such as *European Journal of International Security*, *Security Studies*, *International Relations*, *Nationalism and Ethnic Politics*, *Journal of Peace Research*, *Journal of International Relations and Development*, *Security Dialogue*, *Cooperation and Conflict*, and *Foreign Policy Analysis*.

Leah Sherwood has 17 years of experience in the areas of strategic, human and international security, which was largely gained by working in universities, think tanks, and various government and semi-government entities. Currently, she works at the Department of Defence in Canada where she builds upon her earlier experience at the Privy Council. Previously, she worked in the Middle East and Africa in positions such as Nuclear Security Training Specialist with Emirates Nuclear Energy Corporation, Deputy Director of Research at Trends Research and Advisory (an Abu Dhabi-based think tank specialised in security issues), and Senior Officer at Khalifa University's Institute for International and Civil Security. She has also worked at the Council for Scientific and Industrial Research in Pretoria as a Researcher working on good governance and post-conflict management issues. She has a Ph.D. in International Relations from King's College London and serves as a Fellow at the Middle East and North Africa Forum at Cambridge University.

Hanna Tuominen is a university lecturer and Director of the master's programme in European and Nordic studies at the University of Helsinki. Her research has focused on the values of the European Union (human rights, rule of law), Finnish and EU foreign policy, and EU-UN relations. Her latest research projects have analysed Finnish UN politics and the role and relevance of values in the EU. She has published articles in various academic journals including *The Journal of Common Market Studies, The Hague Journal of Diplomacy, The Nordic Journal of Human Rights* and *Cooperation and Conflict.*

Contents

Introduction

NAMAN KARL-THOMAS HABTOM

In the popular imagination, neutrality is understood as a policy of refraining from joining wars and/or preferring not to choose one bloc or another. This perception, particularly in Western countries, is heavily informed by the experiences of the Second World War (1939–45) and the subsequent Cold War (1947–91), especially as it manifested itself in Europe. In reality, neutrality is a complex and dynamic phenomenon. It ranges from 'active' to 'passive' forms, permanent to non-permanent, as well as various shades that technically are not neutrality but often grouped with it, such as military non-alignment.

The end of the Cold War, and the emergence of the prospect of American unipolarity, led countries around the world to reconsider what neutrality meant, as well as its necessity. For some, this meant a diminished significance and a gradual abandonment of the idea, since neutrality had previously been underpinned by a bipolar world that no longer existed. Following the start of the full-scale Russia-Ukraine conflict in February 2022, the non-aligned (yet often still incorrectly called 'neutral') Sweden and Finland applied to join the North Atlantic Treaty Organization (NATO) – and later completed their accessions – signalling yet another decline in neutrality's role in the twenty-first century.

However, the story of neutrality is not limited to Europe. This is especially true in the post-Cold War era. While the 1990s and the 2000s represented US (and broader Western) hegemony, the 2010s and 2020s have been marked by a growing multipolarity. As the number of rising powers increases, the desire to hedge and refrain from aligning fully with one great power has grown. As a result, while Western observers often remark on the irrelevance and/or death of neutrality, the story is very different elsewhere. This book hopes to illuminate this ongoing development. It seeks to illustrate that neutrality's rise and fall is occurring simultaneously for a plethora of different reasons. In discussing neutrality, this book adopts a wide definition to reflect the broad range of experiences that the countries covered have had and their unique approaches to international affairs.

In the first chapter, Pascal Lottaz examines Switzerland and Austria, the archetypes of neutrality. Despite being externally perceived as similar Alpine neutral states, Lottaz demonstrates that these similarities are in fact superficial. The differences lie both in their histories as well as the underlying philosophies that guide their policies, which in turn continues to affect the way the two understand their own neutrality.

In the second chapter, Erik Noreen and Roxanna Sjöstedt look at Sweden. For decades, the country was seen as the quintessential neutral state that was still engaged in global issues. Even after formally abandoning neutrality as it joined the European Union (EU), the Nordic country pursued a policy of non-alignment. Despite this, as Noreen and Sjöstedt show, Sweden remained a militarily active country, deploying around the world with NATO. The chapter explains how Sweden moved closer to NATO while still officially non-aligned.

In the third chapter, Jussi Pakkasvirta and Hanna Tuominen look at another Nordic neutral, Finland. Following the end of the Cold War, Finnish conceptions of neutrality underwent a major transformation, leading first to Finnish membership in the EU, subsequently to military missions with NATO, and ultimately to NATO membership. Their chapter tracks and analyses this three-decade evolution.

The book's fourth chapter by Karen Devine focuses on Ireland, which has resisted the post-Cold War European trend of military deneutralization. Instead, the country has shown a remarkable resilience and attachment to neutrality despite significant, and growing, pressure from political elites both within and beyond Ireland.

In the second half of the book, in chapters five, six and seven, we leave Europe to see the different ways neutrality is used globally.

In his chapter on Vietnam, Nguyen Khac Giang explains how the southeast Asian nation carries out its 'bamboo diplomacy' as it seeks to balance its relationships with the United States and China while simultaneously seeking out an independent foreign policy.

Israel forms the focus of Liudmila Samarskaia's chapter. Despite being widely seen as an American ally, the Israeli government has at times taken its own path. This has been particularly true in recent years as it seeks to balance its relationship with Washington, Moscow and Beijing in the pursuit of its own national security interests – thereby carrying out a policy of selective neutrality.

Another country associated with neutrality, sometimes called 'the Switzerland of the Middle East', is Oman. In the final chapter of the book, Roby Barrett and Leah Sherwood claim that this perception is incorrect and that Muscat is in fact a partisan non-interventionist. This policy, the authors argue, is in contrast to genuine neutral states and amounts to a *realpolitik* approach that has enabled the country to play the role of a mediator while advancing its own interests.

The countries examined in this volume were selected due to their wide range in interpreting neutrality. They illustrate the fact that neutrality, as interpreted internally or externally, is never a simple or straightforward policy but instead the synthesis of national interests, historical and contemporary circumstances, and domestic and foreign policy realities. As a result, to understand what neutrality is or is not requires a broader view of global developments. By better comprehending these nuances, readers – whether motivated by personal interest, academic research, or policymaking responsibilities – will appreciate that states that practice neutrality and its derivatives do not fit into simple categories, but instead are adapted and perceived by their own traditions and ongoing challenges.

By focusing on the post-Cold War era, this volume seeks to reassert the current relevance of neutrality as a conceptual framework in both international relations and domestic politics. Following the collapse of the Soviet Union and the supposed 'end of history' (Fukuyama 1989), neutrality has in large part been relegated either to history books or viewed as an unconventional quirk/leftover from the Cold War. However, this volume, adding to the works of others, such as Lottaz et al. (2022), illustrates that neutrality – and the imperative to understand its dynamism – remains as important as ever. Neutrality is not simply the product of bipolarity, as the Cold War period may suggest, but can in fact emerge during periods of unipolarity or multipolarity. Additionally, due to the relative uncommonness – albeit not as rare as perhaps popularly imagined – the various manifestations of neutrality are often unique. This requires research into the different forms it takes, or why it is abandoned, which this volume hopes to contribute to.

Neutrality, both as a concept and as a phenomenon, is alive and well. Understanding it, as the chapters in this book seek to do, is crucial as multipolarity becomes a growing force in world affairs. In a world ordered as such, neutrality, in its various forms, will likely continue to be a tool used by various states and recognising it as such helps us comprehend the world both as it exists today and how it may exist tomorrow.

References

Fukuyama, F. 1989. "The End of History?". *The National Interest*. 16, 3–18.

Lottaz, Pascal; Heinz, G; and Herbert, R. R. 2022. *Neutral Beyond the Cold: Neutral States and the Post-Cold War International System*. Lanham: Lexington Books.

1

The Neutralities of Austria and Switzerland: Akin but Not Alike

PASCAL LOTTAZ

Same Packaging, Different Content

Switzerland and Austria are connected not only by a border in the Alps but also by a long-standing and surprisingly intertwined commitment to neutrality. At the Congress of Vienna (1814–1815), the Austrian Empire was one of eight Great Powers giving guarantees for Switzerland's 'perpetual neutrality'. Over a century and two empire-breaking world wars later, the Austrians themselves had to sign a memorandum agreeing to become a neutral state 'like Switzerland' to end the post-war occupation. In recent years, Switzerland used the Austrian example to argue that it could join the United Nations without damaging its neutrality. What goes around comes around. Nevertheless, both states exhibit considerable variances on policy matters. For instance, despite the written promise of the Austrians to follow the Swiss model, one of the first things Vienna did after making neutrality the law of the land was to apply for United Nations (UN) membership – something Switzerland had ruled out for itself, arguing that it would be incompatible with neutrality. In Berne's view, the UN was the club of the winners of World War Two, lacking universality, and was hence off-limits for a neutral state. Similarly, once the Cold War had ended, Austria, together with the northern European neutrals Sweden and Finland, joined the European Union in 1995 – while Switzerland refrained. Although the government and parliament wanted to join the European Economic Community (the EU's precursor), a referendum in 1992 returned a 50.3 per cent no-vote. Swiss critics of European integration have since argued EU membership is incompatible with neutrality – leading to Switzerland's continued absence from the union. Only in 2002 did the country become a UN member, after enough of its people were convinced that the organisation had achieved 'true universality' and thus compatibility with its neutrality.

Austria understands its neutrality in a less limiting way when it comes to participation in international organisations. This is exemplified by various Austrian initiatives, like Chancellor Bruno Kreisky's (1970–83) appeals to resolve the Palestinian question, or more recently Austria's leadership in creating the Treaty on the Prohibition of Nuclear Weapons (TPNW) and its proactive role in facilitating an agreement on Iran's nuclear capabilities (the JCPOA) between Tehran and Washington. Economically and diplomatically, Vienna often understood its foreign policy as what historian Heinz Gärtner (2018) has termed 'engaged neutrality'. In military matters, Vienna also often went different ways, using its neutrality policy as an argument to reduce the size of its forces or advocate for global disarmament and non-proliferation while spending the Cold War straddling the Iron Curtain. In Switzerland, the opposite argument was prominent, that the state needed to maintain a large and heavily equipped army to defend its neutrality against potential threats. Until the late 1960s, Switzerland even contemplated building nuclear weapons – significantly supported by parts of the military establishment who believed only a Swiss bomb could uphold the country's neutrality in the nuclear age (Zogg 2024).

Why is it that on paper it looks as if Switzerland and Austria shared a commitment to the same neutral principles, but in practice they deviate so significantly on concrete policies? This chapter explores the main factors for the differences and similarities in contemporary Austrian and Swiss neutrality conceptions. On the one hand, analogous developments in the early days of both legally guaranteed neutralities partially elucidate why they have more in common with each other than with other neutrals of comparable ages. On the other hand, the differences in Berne's and Vienna's international needs and their individual historical trajectories explain why they both went their own ways in defining this fuzzy concept.

Children of War

Before discussing the differences, let us consider which factors make Swiss and Austrian neutralities look alike. First and foremost, they were both shaped by how different European wars ended, during which both states experienced occupation: For the Swiss, it was the Napoleonic Wars that came with conquest by the French. For the Austrians it was the Second World War and the subsequent Allied occupation. In both cases, their modern-day neutralities were part of a package deal as a post-war settlement.

In 1815, at the Congress of Vienna, the assembled eight Great Powers put down in writing that they 'acknowledged that the general interest demands that the Helvetic States should enjoy the benefit of a perpetual neutrality; and wishing, by territorial restitution and cessions, to enable it to secure its independence and maintain its neutrality' (Hansard, 1816). This landmark treaty, to which Switzerland acceded a few months later, was pivotal in two ways. On the one hand, it neutralised Switzerland under international law and bound the great powers to recognize this status while also adding important state territory to the Helvetic body; Geneva, a corridor leading to it, and Basel would henceforth be part of the nineteen cantons of Switzerland. The Great Powers were in words and deeds interested in making the Swiss body politic a viable part of the European concert system, strong and independent enough to buffer Austria and France, preventing the Alps between them from being used as a staging ground by either side to threaten the other, and ensuring that Switzerland would not again become a vassal-state – as had happened under Napoleon (Bonjour 1978, 42). On the other hand, the inclusion of a 'perpetual neutrality' clause was also a novelty in international law.

Promises of occasional neutrality (maintaining neutrality under certain circumstances toward a partner state) in bilateral treaties have been a staple of European politics since the thirteenth century (Neff 2000). Even imperial Austria would go on to use it during the Crimean War (1853–56), but never before had a state signed up to maintain unconditional neutrality in all future wars. In an age when the power to make war was a prerogative of a sovereign state, this was unheard of and attested to Switzerland's relative weakness. It was, however, based on its own wishes for such an arrangement, mediated by a skilled Genevan diplomat, Charles Pictet de Rochemont, who managed to gain Russia's support to pitch the suggestion to the other powers who then adopted it in the form of a treaty and who understood that Switzerland had to serve European peace in the coming balance of power (Lehmann 2020, 209–216; 333–334).

One hundred and forty years later, it was again the Russians (the Soviets to be precise) who slowly but gradually warmed up to the idea of settling another alpine question – this time, defeated Austria – by way of a neutrality agreement. Again, the arrangement had a very strong geopolitical component, as the Soviets above all wanted to forestall Austria from joining the young NATO alliance. But the four-way occupation (the Soviet Union, the United States, Britain, and France) of the country made it impossible to integrate Austria completely into the Soviet orbit as Stalin had done elsewhere. Hence, a nonaligned buffer state between the Soviet and US spheres of influence started to look reasonable when the occupations of both Austria and Germany dragged on, especially after Moscow started to understand that Austria might serve as a template for solving the German question – an outcome that did not materialise but influenced Soviet decision-making (Gehler 2015).

The Austrian government delegation that visited Moscow in April 1955, sensing the shift in the Kremlin's attitude, convinced General Secretary Nikita Khrushchev to accept an Austrian neutrality 'like Switzerland' in return for an end to Soviet (and other Allied nations) occupation. The Soviets even agreed to make this only an informal understanding between the diplomatic representatives in the form of a memorandum instead of a hard clause in the State Treaty that restored Austrian sovereignty a month later. This was a point of considerable importance to Vienna. Its delegates did not want to be 'neutralised' through an international agreement but to choose the policy of their own free will. They dutifully lived up to their promise, as on 26 October 1955, the Austrian parliament passed a constitutional law making their state perpetually neutral. Vienna subsequently notified all states that it was in diplomatic contact with of its new status, asking for their active acceptance or passive acknowledgment. The country's foremost legal scholars count this as the beginning of Austria's neutral status under international law (Schreiner 2018, 41).

In both cases, it was a combination of Great Power willingness to accept a neutral solution together with a defeated nation's willingness to promise permanent neutrality that finally cleared the way for a neutral solution to a great power contest.

Bound By Their Own Laws

This brings us to a second important similarity – for both states, the internationally recognized characters of their neutralities led to their codification into national legislation. Switzerland enshrined it in two key paragraphs of its 1848 constitution, the founding document of modern-day Switzerland. Although the wording slightly changed over time, the principles of the paragraphs remained the same. They oblige the legislative and executive branches of the state (the National Assembly and the Federal Council) to maintain the 'external security, independence, and neutrality' of the state (Art. 173 and 185). This does not make neutrality part of the national objectives, as the federal administration has insisted repeatedly (Motion 05.3213), but it does elevate it to a principle of foreign policy to which both branches of government are bound (Interpellation 14.3331). A similar obligation is put on the Austrian state through a federal constitutional law (Bundesverfassungsgesetz, 1955):

> (1) For the purpose of asserting its independence to the outside world and for the purpose of safeguarding the inviolability of its territory, Austria voluntarily declares its perpetual neutrality. Austria will maintain and defend this neutrality using all means at its disposal.

(2) Austria will not enter into any military alliances in order to secure these purposes in the future, and it will not allow the establishment of military bases of foreign states on its territory.

This provision even defines Austrian neutrality to some extent, which is lacking in the Swiss case. Regardless, the fact that both constitutions mention neutrality is a domestic legal aspect differentiating the Alpine nations from other neutrals of similar periods that used neutrality policy merely as a tool in the absence of better options. The prime examples are Sweden and Finland, which never had explicit neutrality provisions in their national laws. The Swedes had been neutral like Switzerland since 1815, but not because of an agreement with foreign powers. They simply did not join any wars or alliances for 200 years. They even tried to create a Scandinavian defence alliance several times before and after World War II. It was the failure of those endeavours and the lack of alternatives that led the Swedes back to neutrality several times. Finland, too, started calling its foreign policy neutral out of necessity after having lost World War Two and having been forced into a security arrangement with the USSR. For Helsinki, calling their foreign policy neutral was a way of resisting Soviet demands for closer integration – much to the chagrin of Moscow, which until the Gorbachev era did not agree to call the Finns neutral (Juntunen 2024).

However, like Stockholm, Helsinki never actually codified its neutrality in national legislation, nor did it seek the status of a permanent neutral under international law like Austria. Both Nordic states were following pragmatic neutrality policies geared toward specific security predicaments. While the Finns had to be careful of their relationship with the USSR and thus followed a policy beneficial to Moscow (in the West pejoratively referred to as 'Finlandization'), the Swedes were leaning their security thinking heavily on the West, or, as Mikael af Malmborg (2001, 52) explains, 'anyone with the slightest acquaintance with Swedish military planning (...) knew that there was never talk of more than one enemy' – i.e. the Soviet Union.

Consequently, it was relatively simple for both Nordic states to discard their neutral positions after the Cold War. Once the East-West dichotomy had ceased and the threat level declined, Sweden and Finland first reframed their foreign policies around the turn of the millennium as 'non-alignment in peacetime', discarding references to hard neutrality in their foreign policy communication – and ultimately, gave up also on that stance in 2022 when they applied for NATO membership. Unlike when Sweden joined the EU, this step was achieved without a long and hard public debate since no public referendum was needed to change their constitutions or national laws. This aspect differs strongly from Switzerland and Austria, both of which would face much larger public hurdles to change the policy, as that would necessitate an extensive involvement of the general public for the sake of changing such a fundamental element of national identity. In Austria, a two-thirds majority in both chambers of parliament would be needed to change the neutrality law. An even bigger hurdle exists for Switzerland, where changes to the constitution can only be achieved through a mandatory referendum. In this regard, the Alpine neutralities have always been more firmly rooted in domestic law than their Nordic counterparts.

Neutrality Provides Identity

Lastly, in both countries, the discourse about the fundamental principles of the state led to the identification of large parts of the population with it. People perceive neutrality as an essential part of what it means to be Austrian or Swiss. At different times but in similar ways, private citizens, politicians, and thinkers started attributing values to neutrality that went well beyond a simple foreign policy. For instance, Pictet de Rochemont, the aforementioned nineteenth century Swiss diplomat and one of the intellectual fathers of modern Swiss neutrality, viewed the policy as a service to Europe, allowing for the establishment of lasting peace by guarding the Alps against Great Power competition. This idea impacted many contemporary liberals to rethink Switzerland's position in the nation-building process of that age as an inherently European project. A century later, the experience of having survived two world wars unharmed had another deep impact on the national psyche, convincing generations of Swiss that policies of self-defense and self-reliance – neutrality included – were right to protect their livelihoods inside a small state. Neutrality had become itself a value and an identity that needed to be maintained (Fischer & Möckli 2016).

Hence, Cold War Swiss discourse was centred around the perils of being part of foreign efforts to consolidate power away from the state, like European integration or the UN. Much of this was firmly rooted in popular beliefs about fundamental Swiss values. Consistently, opinion polls came out with astronomical approval rates for neutrality – even after the Cold War. Since 1989, the Center for Security Studies in Zürich conducts yearly surveys on popular opinion about various security issues, showing an unwavering approval for maintaining neutrality between 80 and 97 percent. Although the Russo-Ukrainian War in 2022 led to a 'plummeting' of those values from 97 per cent to 89 per cent, they have since gone up again to 91 per cent in 2023 (Szvircsev Tresch et al., 2023). If anything, the end of the Cold War made neutrality only more appealing to the Swiss populace.

The same is true for Austria, where neutrality has become an important part of national identity. For instance, 26 October, the day Austria passed its neutrality act, is today celebrated as the republic's national day. The decision to adopt a holiday to celebrate the Austrian state was taken in 1965. For the entirety of the Cold War it was celebrated under the name 'Day of Neutrality'. This contrasts with other national holidays like the United States' Independence Day or Germany's Day of German Unity, and reflects how strongly neutrality was part of Austria's emerging national identity. Although this tradition has been changing in recent years (Schreiner 2018, pp. 225–229), the identification of Austrian statehood with neutrality is still fundamental, enunciated most recently by the speeches of the President of the Republic Alexander van der Bellen and Minister of Defense Klaudia Tanner in their addresses to the nation on 26 October 2022. Although Chancellor Karl Nehammer did not mention neutrality in his speech, Van der Bellen (2022) and Tanner (2022) called it a 'principle' giving Austrians a sense of orientation and a 'high value'. Consequently, as in Switzerland, neutrality has remained extremely popular among the public also after the Cold War, with most approval rates hovering between 60–80 per cent, depending on the year and questions asked. Even in 2023, only 16 per cent of Austrians wanted to join NATO while 71 per cent preferred remaining neutral (Gallup 2023).

Blurry Origins versus New Beginnings

There are, however, fundamental differences in the normative developments of the two neutrality conceptions that partially explain the observable variations on the policy level. To begin with, the origins of the two neutralities are remembered differently. In this regard, the two nations are as different as it gets. Austria became a small state in the heart of the Alps only after being defeated in two world wars. The Second Republic that emerged after World War Two was a far cry from the vast, multi-ethnic, multilingual empire that Vienna once controlled. This experience is radically different from Switzerland, which was not fighting in either war and had been a small alpine republic for centuries, tracing its statehood back to 1291. The Austrian trauma of being reduced from a Great Power to a small state leaves little space for narratives of historical continuity. The Austria of the nineteenth century is a memory of a long bygone past, not part of today's lived experience. Even 'modern Switzerland', meaning the political order founded in 1848, is 100 years older than the Second Republic. Hence, when it comes to identity, the Swiss claim much older origins of their contemporary statehood and foundational national policies. This is especially pertinent for the neutrality debate.

In fact, there are long-running debates about the origins of Swiss neutrality. Since the early twentieth century, historians (e.g. Bonjour 1946; Lyon 1960; Sherman 1918) inside and outside of Switzerland date neutrality not to 1815 but to the Battle of Marignano in 1515 where the Confederate forces were decisively beaten by the French. It was through that defeat, the argument goes, that the Swiss had learned their lesson to remain outside of European great power politics – and instead of fighting in foreign wars, to practice an even older tradition of 'sitting still'. While Marignano was indeed an important moment in Swiss history, there is no consensus around whether the battle should be considered as the beginning of the neutrality policy (see Bugmann 2000 and Nünlist 2017). The tradition of Swiss mercenaries serving foreign kings did not cease – to this day the Vatican still employs the last remnants of that practice – nor did a coherent foreign policy among the different cantons follow from it. It was rather the mutual defence agreements, the so-called 'Defensionals' among the cantons that followed in the late sixteenth and seventeenth centuries that were more important, as they bound the loosely connected confederate cantons together militarily for strictly defensive purposes, hence making an offensive use of Swiss soldiers or an alliance with foreign powers much less likely. However, the Helvetic construct of mostly sovereign cantons was so weak and heterogeneous that until the late eighteenth century there were serious doubts within the confederation if it was even a viable national project (Holenstein 2019). Still, the idea that Switzerland 'has been neutral since Marignano' (Maissen 2018) is widespread and popular not only among national conservative circles. Even the Swiss Government in a 1993 booklet on 'The Neutrality of Switzerland' distributed by the federal administration until 2022, traced Switzerland's neutrality timeline back to 1515. Before, during, and after the Cold War, the Swiss seem hard set on claiming a 500-year-old tradition.

Austria is completely different in this respect. There are no mythical origin stories or romantic memories of the old days. For most Austrians, it is even a surprise to learn that their empire had brushes with neutrality before the twentieth century, during the Crimean War. There are no attempts of connecting the policy of 1955 with older principles relating to Austrian history or pre-World War identity. On the contrary, Austrian neutrality was part of a much-needed new beginning after forty years of identity-shattering events, from the loss of empire to the direct collaboration with Nazism and genocide. This is well visible looking at the way neutrality has been glorified as more than just a foreign policy but a status under international law – a way for Austria to exist in the international community. Hence, the national day celebrations that revolve around neutrality are no coincidence. Neutrality was consciously elevated to a fundamental principle of the state, something each and every Austrian ought to be aware of. In 1965, there were other options to choose from for a national day, but parliament decided explicitly to use neutrality as the focal point of national identity. Socio-psychological factors might have played a role in this but, at least in part, it was a conscious political decision for the sake of building a new Austrian identity after a painful cut with the past.

The Dogmatic Fork in The Early Cold War

Another fundamental difference is the conceptualization of what concrete foreign policies of a small permanent neutral state should look like. A 'dogmatic split' with far-reaching consequences occurred in the 1950s, from the very beginning of Austrian neutrality. Two prominent and respected international law thinkers were the theoreticians of the split: Rudolf Bindschedler of Switzerland and Alfred Verdross of Austria. Although neither was the originator of the political approaches – those decisions had been made previously – they enunciated them in jurisprudential terms influencing generations of Swiss and Austrian thinkers until now. Their interpretations of neutrality became so prominent that academics and officials literally started using the word "doctrine" to refer to their respective theses.

In 1954, Bindschedler, who had been working as an in-house lawyer for the Political Department (Switzerland's Ministry of Foreign Affairs), wrote a short four-page memo on the meaning of neutrality. Although it never became the official position of the Federal Council, the memo was widely circulated in the administration and referred to throughout the Cold War. He established the idea that permanent neutrals, due to their obligation to remain neutral in all future wars, were under special, secondary obligations during peacetime to make sure none of their foreign policy decisions would make neutrality impossible during wartime. This line of thinking developed into the so-called *Vorwirkungslehre* (doctrine of preconditions) according to which the status of permanent neutrality came with preconditions that needed to be fulfilled by way of a correct peacetime neutrality policy in addition to maintaining strict legal neutrality when war broke out. One such precondition was (for obvious reasons) not to join a military alliance. But just as important was not being part of economic or political clubs that could force their members to commit 'unneutral' actions during wartime. Bindschedler phrased it as follows:

> When participating in international conferences and organisations, it is important to distinguish whether they have a predominantly political, economic, cultural, or technical aspect. If they are conferences or organisations of a political nature, participation can only be considered if they exhibit a certain universality. The main representatives of the relevant political groups must participate, especially both parties involved in any potential conflict. Also in this respect it is important for Switzerland to avoid taking sides (Bindschedler, 1954).

The Bindschedler Doctrine line of thinking was one of the main reasons Switzerland stayed away from UN membership until 2002 (Fischer and Möckli 2016).

A distinctly different theory of permanent neutrality was formulated by Alfred Verdross, a dean of the law faculty at the University of Vienna and one of the country's foremost experts in international law. In conjunction with his colleague, Laurenz Kunz, he held that not only was it in the discretion of the Security Council to exempt member states from participating in military coercive measures, but that UN members had acknowledged Austria's status as a permanent neutral by virtue of being notified thereof. Furthermore, Austria's intention to join the UN was part of the State Treaty which was then signed by 4 of the 5 permanent members of the Security Council. Verdross interpreted this as more evidence of the UN taking note of Austria's new status and that this would oblige the Security Council to allow Austria's adherence to neutrality law if a conflict should break out. Although both men recognized that the collective security principle of the UN was somewhat at odds with the principle of neutrality, they also argued that both aimed at the same goal, namely protecting peace and international security, and that the contradiction was hence only one of means but not one of ends, and thus could co-exist (Schreiner 2018, 32–34). In essence, the central tenet of the Verdross doctrine was to give precedence to the responsibilities of neutrality over the responsibilities of solidarity within the collective security system. This understanding of the interplay between neutrality and collective security became the dominant viewpoint in the field of international law and still shapes Austria's approach to foreign policy today (Senn 2023, 33–34).

Neutrality Changing or Disappearing?

For the above dogmatic and ideological reasons, Swiss foreign policy during the Cold War remained focused for a long time on maintaining as much independence as possible in security, economic, and political terms. It was not an isolationist policy like that of Albania, or a nonaligned stance in the way Yugoslavia started developing it. Switzerland participated in key elements of the West's Cold War economic structure like the Marshall Plan (starting in 1947) and later unofficially cooperated with COCOM export controls, bringing Switzerland into the Euro-Atlantic trade system. Neither did Bern oppose diplomatic participation in universal but non-binding pan-European endeavours like the Council of Europe, which it joined in 1963. Also, together with Europe's other neutral and non-aligned states, it played an important role in creating the Conference on Security and Cooperation in Europe (CSCE) in the mid-1970s (Fischer 2009). Furthermore, Switzerland remained willing to support international peace and diplomacy activities when asked to do so. It was part of two neutral commissions implementing the Korean armistice after 1953. It also remained willing to provide Geneva as a European meeting ground for the UN and a plethora of other international organisations. Finally, there is Bern's long-standing practice of providing good office services to mediate between third states that broke relations. Some of these efforts remained low-key, while others became visible, as during the Iran hostage crisis of 1979–80, the 1985 superpower summits in Geneva (Fischer and Möckli 2016) and, more recently, the mediation efforts between Russia and Georgia in 2010–11 and the 2021 US-Russia summit in Geneva.

However, on issues touching directly on military affairs and political independence, Bern has been maintaining an arms-length distance. Whenever supranational organisations and the pooling of sovereignty are involved, the Bindschedler understanding of neutrality influenced the political debate – albeit this inclination gradually decreased after the Cold War. Some activities, especially the ones of military nature, have been prompted by the changed nature of the international system. Even after Russia joined NATO's Partnership for Peace (PfP) program in 1994, the Swiss also started cooperating in that format from 1996 – there was no more danger of being one-sided. Switzerland also contributed troops to the KFOR mission established in accordance with UN Security Council Resolution 1244 (the peace plan for Kosovo) starting from 1999. Although the step was emotionally debated inside Switzerland and opposed by national conservatives, the fact that the resolution had the backing even of Yugoslavia meant that at least on paper, the universality of the mission was given in addition to its peacekeeping nature. Then, in 2002, Switzerland joined the UN and over the next 20 years, gradually reduced also its reservations toward NATO, to the point that in 2023 the Federal Council published a new security doctrine (Zusatzbericht 2022) which explicitly says that cooperation with the alliance is pivotal to the point that even 'interoperability' is mentioned as an objective.

The plan is to allow for joint defence of Switzerland in case of an attack by an outside force – in which case all neutrality laws would cease to apply. Post-Cold War Switzerland thus seems to have fewer reservations toward collaboration in EU politics than before. It joined several EU-led policy schemes like the Schengen agreement for visa-free travel (joining in 2008). However, not all is clear on this trajectory. In 2021, the negotiations for a framework agreement that the EU wanted to negotiate with the Swiss as a fundament for future cooperation was rejected by Bern, leading to the deepest crisis in Swiss-EU relations in decades as the EU is unwilling to negotiate new bilateral agreements without the framework.

Which direction Switzerland's sovereign and neutral path in Europe will take is anything but clear. This is also illustrated by a popular initiative that wants to force a public referendum on whether economic sanctions should be part of Swiss neutrality, or not. After the breakout of full-scale warfare in Ukraine on February 24, 2022, the Swiss government declared that it would impose the same sanctions as the EU did on Russia. This was not a breach of neutrality, the Federal Council argued, because it was a sovereign decision and not breaching the letter of neutrality law, nor its track-record of the last 30 years. Switzerland had applied wartime sanctions for the first time on Iraq in 1990, in reaction to its invasion of Kuwait. Henceforth, the Federal Council applied sanctions several times, as in 2014 in the reaction to Russia's annexation of Crimea. Each time, Bern's approach to sanctions became more partisan. In the Iraqi case, sanctions had at least been ordered by the UN. In 2014 Switzerland implemented sanctions similar to those the EU imposed on Russia (but Berne still defined the content of the sanctions by itself). Finally, in 2022, it simply copied the same sanctions the EU levied on Russia.

Thus, sanctions were not only a Post-Cold War issue but also one that increased in its partisan character over time – all while Switzerland defended the view that sanctions are compatible with its legalistic understanding of neutrality. But the national conservative People's Party disagrees. Considering that US president Joe Biden (2022) said about the sanctions that 'even Switzerland' had joined them, they view the credibility of neutrality as under threat. Legal neutrality helps little, they say, when warfare is implemented through economic measures. Therefore, together with supporters from the left, they initiated a process to force a referendum on the sanctions issue in the form of a new constitutional definition of Swiss neutrality. In early 2024 this succeeded in gathering the required 100,000 signatures to become a referendum that will be held in 2027 or 2028.

Austria, as we have seen, was and still is much less hesitant when it comes to reconciling neutrality with international integration. Like Switzerland, it was partially integrated with COCOM export controls but had one of the highest trade volumes of West European states with the East (Luif 1984). Bruno Kreisky, the popular and long-serving Social Democratic chancellor of the 1970s, implemented what he called an 'active neutrality', which saw him engaging in dynamic third-party diplomacy, promoting multilateralism, supporting the process of détente between the East and West, and getting involved in North-South disputes, even proposing a so-called 'Marshall Plan for the Third World'. Kreisky also strongly advocated for the rights of Palestinians and collaborated with the German and Swedish Social Democratic leaders, Willy Brandt and Olof Palme, on issues of international socialism (Gärtner 2018). Such proactive initiatives set Austria's diplomacy apart from the much more reactive foreign policy of Switzerland during the Cold War.

While some of these activities are influenced by individual personalities, the more engaged character of the Austrian approach is visible also after the end of the Cold War when Vienna joined the EU – and thereby also became a member of its Common Foreign and Security Policy (CFSP) and Common Security and Defence Policy (CSDP). In 1998 and 2010, the national parliament adopted another constitutional law that such EU policies were not a breach of the 1955 neutrality law. Since neither the CFSP nor the CSDP amount to an alliance commitment, Austria, like all other EU member states, has a de facto veto over the creation of alliance-like mechanisms in these areas because decisions have to be unanimous. In addition, the provisions of an opt-out for neutral states (the 'Irish-clause'), means that maintaining neutrality even during an armed attack on the EU, is still possible even if the CSDP collective defence article should be triggered (Hauser 2020).

The more proactive nature of Austrian neutrality in comparison to the Swiss version was showcased again in April 2022, when Chancellor Karl Nehammer became the first EU head of state to visit Moscow and talk directly to Russian President Vladimir Putin after the invasion of Ukraine. Like Switzerland, Austria is part of the sanctions regime against Russia but has so far resisted sending weapons to Ukraine. On the other hand, it has allowed military transports through its territory and made monetary contributions to the Orwellian-sounding 'European Peace Facility' which has been financing weapon systems for use by Ukraine against Russia (Janik 2022).

Conclusion

The neutralities of Austria and Switzerland might look alike and have influenced each other for a long time, but under the hood, they are different animals, philosophically and practically. That should not be all too surprising because, after all, they are different countries with different historical trajectories and different challenges to master. Hence, they adapted their neutrality principles and foreign policies to their own needs. In this process, country-specific developments matter as much as the common experiences of the two states. To the Austrians, the status of neutrality is part of a new beginning, while to the Swiss it is a connection to a mythological past. Hence, political rhetoric about the concept differs today as one is prone to emphasise the importance of neutrality for regaining independence while the other portrays it as something that has guaranteed its sovereignty throughout the centuries and which it had to defend several times.

In the Cold War, Swiss and Austrian neutralities looked different because one understood the principle as meaning little or no participation in international structures, while the other did not. The difference is not induced by the neutrality concept itself but rather by the experience of prior years, leading local thinkers, politicians, and the public to fill the neutrality concept with meanings suiting their conceptions about that past. The difference melts away if we compare not the contemporary neutrality concepts but the progression thereof. Switzerland in 1815, at the beginning of its guaranteed permanent neutrality, had no problem connecting its status with the security of Europe – as Pictet de Rochemont did – and even in 1919 it still saw no contradiction in joining the League of Nations. Early Swiss conceptions of permanent neutrality resemble early Austrian conceptions of the same; they only change over time as new wars shaped new experiences about the neutrality concept.

That is why there are some strange contradictions between the two. While Austria is forbidden from joining a military alliance by its own constitution, it does not view the EU or the CSDP as such and is hence perfectly able to reconcile neutrality with EU integration. Switzerland, on the other hand, does not (yet) have a hard prohibition against joining a military alliance in its constitution, but large parts of the population view EU sovereignty-pooling and the CSDP as incompatible with how they understand neutrality. This is a position strongly influenced by the Cold War definitions that became popular decades ago. Unless either or both states will follow in the footsteps of Sweden and Finland, giving up their neutralities completely, this process will probably continue. New wars will keep shaping the understanding of what neutrality means to the Swiss and the Austrians and impact the policies of their governments. Likely, they will not be the same.

References

PRIMARY SOURCES

Bundespräsident Alexander van der Bellen. "Bundespräsident mahnt in seiner TV-Ansprache zu integrer Politik und ruft zu Zuversicht in Zeiten multipler Krisen auf." Accessed June 28, 2023. https://www.bundespraesident.at/aktuelles/detail/tv-ansprache-1

Bundesverfassungsgesetz vom 26. Oktober 1955 über die Neutralität Österreichs. StF: BGBl. Nr. 211/1955

Biden, Joseph R."Remarks of President Joe Biden – State of the Union Address As Prepared for Delivery." The White House, March 1, 2022. Accessed July 19, 2023. https://www.whitehouse.gov/briefing-room/speeches-remarks/2022/03/01/remarks-of-president-joe-biden-state-of-the-union-address-as-delivered

Tanner, Klaudia. "Nationalfeiertag 2022." NYC Mayor's Office. Streamed live on January 10, 2019. YouTube video, 2:23:22. https://www.youtube.com/live/59GlYo30EqY?feature=share

SNC Motion 05.3213. Ernst Schibli, "Bessere Verankerung der Neutralität in der Verfassung." Swiss Naitonal Council, March 18, 2005. Accessed July 19, 2023. https://www.parlament.ch/de/ratsbetrieb/suche-curia-vista/geschaeft?AffairId=20053213

SNC Interpellation 14.3331. Hans Fehr, "Ukraine-Krise. Schweizerische Neutralität oder Annäherung an die Nato?" Swiss National Council, May 8, 2014. Accessed July 19, 2023. https://www.parlament.ch/de/ratsbetrieb/suche-curia-vista/geschaeft?AffairId=20143331

"Zusatzbericht zum Sicherheitspolitischen Bericht 2021 über die Folgen des Krieges in der Ukraine" Swiss Federal Council, September 7, 2022. Accessed July 21, 2023. https://www.fedlex.admin.ch/eli/fga/2022/2357/de

SECONDARY SOURCES

Bindschedler, R. 1954. "Der Begriff der Neutralität". In S. Zala (Ed.), *Diplomatic Documents of Switzerland*. Dodis. dodis.ch/9564.

Bonjour, E. 1946. *Swiss Neutrality: Its History and Meaning* (M. Hottinger, Trans.). Routledge.

Bonjour, E. 1978. *Geschichte der schweizerischen Neutralität : Kurzfassung* [History of Swiss Neutrality : Condensed Version]. Helbing & Lichtenhahn.

Bugmann, U. 2000. "How to Create a National Myth: Switzerland Reflected in its Contemporary Writing". In M. Butler, M. Pender, & J. Charnley (Eds.), *The Making of Modern Switzerland, 1848–1998*. MacMillan.

Eidgenössisches Departement für Verteidigung, B. u. S. V. 2014. *Die Neutralität der Schweiz* (4 ed.). Schweizerische Eidgenossenschaft.

Fischer, T. 2009. *Neutral Power in the CSCE – The N+N States and the Making of the Helsinki Accords 1975*. Nomos for the Austrian Institute for International Affairs.

Fischer, T., & Möckli, D. 2016. "The Limits of Compensation: Swiss Neutrality Policy in the Cold War". *Journal of Cold War Studies*. *18*, 12-35. https://doi.org/10.1162/JCWS_a_00678

Gallup. 2023. *Gallup Stimmungsbarometer: Zwei-Länder-Umfrage zum Thema Neutralität: Österreich und Schweiz*. Gallup Institut.

Gärtner, H. 2018. "Austria: Engaged Neutrality". In A. Cottey (Ed.), *The European Neutrals and NATO*. 129–150. Palgrave MacMillan.

Gehler, M. 2015. *Modellfall für Deutschland? Die Österreichlösung mit Staatsvertrag und Neutralität 1945–1955*. StudienVerlag.

Hansard, T. C. (Ed.). 1816. *The Parliamentary Debates from the Year 1803 to the Present Time*. Vol. 37. T.C. Hansard.

Hauser, G. 2020. "Neutral and Nonaligned States in the European Union". In H. Reginbogin & P. Lottaz (Eds.), *Permanent Neutrality: A Model for Peace, Security, and Justice*. 111–128. Lexington Books.

Holenstein, A. 2019. "Miliz im Reformstau. Das Scheitern einer nationalen Verteidigungsorganisation als Spiegel der schweizerischen Integrationsblockade im späten Ancien Régime". In P. Rogger & R. Schmid Keeling (Eds.), *Miliz oder Söldner? : Wehrpflicht und Solddienst in Stadt, Republik und Fürstenstaat 13.–18. Jahrhundert*. 173–191. Brill. https://doi.org/https://doi.org/10.30965/9783657792580_010

Janik, R. 2022. "Neutralität und der österreichische Beitrag zur EU-Sicherheitspolitik". *ÖGfE Policy Brief* (14/2022), 1–10.

Juntunen, T. 2024. "Finland: From Curious Observer to Active Accommodator of the NPT Process". In P. Lottaz & Y. Iwama (Eds.), *Neutral Europe and the Creation of the Nonproliferation Regime 1958–68*. Routledge.

Lehmann, P. 2020. *Die Umdeutung der Neutralität: Eine politische Ideengeschichte der Eidgenossenschaft vor und nach 1815*. Schwab Verlag.

Luif, P. 1984. "Embargoes in East-West Trade and the European Neutrals: The Case of Austria". *Current Research on Peace and Violence*. 7(4), 221–228.

Lyon, P. 1960. "Neutrality and the Emergence of the Concept of Neutralism". *The Review of Politics*, *22*(2), 255–268. http://www.jstor.org.libproxy.temple. edu/stable/1405320

Maissen, T. 2018. Seit wann ist die Schweiz "neutral seit Marignano"? Zu den Wurzeln eines nationalpädagogischen Topos. *Schweizerische Zeitschrift für Geschichte*. *68*(2), 214–239.

Malmborg, M. a. 2001. *Neutrality and State-building in Sweden*. Palgrave.

Neff, S. C. 2000. *The Rights and Duties of Neutrals: A General History*. Manchester University Press.

Nünlist, C. 2017. "Neutrality for Peace: Switzerland's Independent Foreign Policy". In H. Gärtner (Ed.), *Engaged Neutrality* (pp. 161–187). Lexington Books.

Schreiner, J. 2018. *Neutralität nach "Schweizer Muster"? Österreichische Völkerrechtslehre zur immerwährenden Neutralität, 1955–1989*. Nomos.

Senn, M. 2023. "Österreichs Neutralität". In M. Senn, F. Eder, & M. Kornprobst (Eds.), *Handbuch Außenpolitik Österreichs*. 23–50. Springer.

Sherman, G. E. 1918. "The Neutrality of Switzerland I". *The American Journal of International Law*. *12*(2), 241–250. https://doi.org/https://doi. org/10.2307/2188141

Szvircsev Tresch, T., Wenger, A., De Rosa, S., Ferst, T., Rizzo, E., Robert, J., & Roost, T. 2023. *Sicherheit 2023: Aussen-, Sicherheits- und Verteidigungspolitische Meinungsbildung im Trend*. Center for Security Studies.

Zogg, B. 2024. "Switzerland: The Nuclear Path And The NPT". In P. Lottaz & Y. Iwama (Eds.), *Neutral Europe and the Creation of the Nonproliferation Regime 1958–68*. Routledge.

2

Sweden's Role in International Security Affairs: Officially Non-Aligned but Ready to Serve

ERIK NOREEN AND ROXANNA SJÖSTEDT

Although Sweden is a small state in terms of both population, economic impact, and military powers, its foreign and security policy has always been characterised by high international ambitions and a strong desire to impact world affairs. Since the 1920s, Sweden has advocated the joining of international organisations, such as the League of Nations and subsequently the United Nations, to actively participate in, as well as influence, international relations. It has consistently maintained a strategic narrative that combines national priorities with international aspirations, particularly during times of different forms of global conflict, such as World War Two or the Cold War. During the Cold War, national priorities were guided by two key aspects. Firstly, the overarching ideology of 'non-alignment in peace aiming at neutrality in war' was a central pillar of Sweden's foreign policy. This ideology sought to preserve neutrality and independence during times of conflict. Secondly, Sweden has recognized the importance of maintaining a relatively strong defence capability to defend against potential invasions. Sweden's policy of 'small state realism' played a significant role in domestic politics, helping to neutralise criticism from both the political left and right (Dalsjö 2010b, 63). This policy aimed to strike a balance between maintaining neutrality and engaging in internationalism. Sweden actively participated in the United Nations, particularly on issues related to disarmament, and was vocal in criticising major powers when they committed acts of aggression against smaller states (Bjereld 1995, 23–35).

However, words and actions did not always align. When the Swedish military archives were opened following the end of the Cold War, a substantial amount of information revealed that Sweden's policy of neutrality had not been as strong or consistent as the Swedish people had been led to believe. Since the

1940s, Sweden had been actively preparing for extensive cooperation with NATO, especially in coordination with the Nordic NATO countries. A Danish investigation accurately described Sweden's strategy during this period as 'a declared non-alignment combined with close collaboration with Western countries' (Holmström 2023, 33).

The post-Cold War era brought about significant changes and new possibilities for Sweden in the international arena. With the dissolution of the Soviet Union, Sweden no longer saw the need to maintain a strict policy of neutrality, and the absence of power blocs allowed for a reassessment of the Swedish position and the exploration of new security policy avenues. As a result, Swedish government officials began to describe their country as a European state, and Sweden eventually joined the European Union (EU) in 1995. Another notable change was the alteration of Sweden's foreign policy declarations. The policy of neutrality was removed and replaced with the concept of 'military non-alignment' (Ministry for Foreign Affairs 1992, 30). This shift signalled a departure from strict neutrality and a willingness to engage in military cooperation and partnerships. Consequently, Sweden joined the NATO-initiated Partnership for Peace program (PfP). PfP was designed to promote cooperation and dialogue between NATO and non-NATO countries, allowing for military collaboration and interoperability without formal membership in the alliance (Dalsjö 2010b, 68).

The post-Cold War security policy shift culminated in the first decade of the new millennium. Firstly, in the early 2000s, the Swedish Armed Forces (SAF) underwent a transformation regarding defence strategy. This emphasised a transition from a traditional defence posture – focusing on repelling a potential invasion – to a more flexible defence approach centred on international missions and cooperative security efforts (Dalsjö 2010b, 66–70). Secondly, SAF transitioned from a conscription-based organisation to a smaller volunteer force. This shift led to a significant reduction in the number of soldiers that could be mobilised in times of war. Despite becoming a member of the European Union in 1995, full membership in NATO appeared politically challenging during the early 2000s, with public support for NATO membership ranging from 22 to 29 per cent in opinion polls between 2002 and 2013 (Bjereld and Oscarsson 2023, 8). The annexation of Crimea by Russia in 2014 had a noticeable impact on public opinion regarding this matter. Furthermore, with a government decision in December 2014, the obligation to conduct conscript training was revived, and in January 2018, regiments began to receive conscripts after conscription training was reactivated (Löfven 2017). Against the backdrop of Russia's increasingly aggressive policies towards Ukraine, culminating in a full Russian invasion in 2022, Sweden shifted its security policy completely towards a focus on investing in defence against invasion and a national perspective at the expense of international engagements. After the relatively unsuccessful missions in Afghanistan and Mali, Sweden was not involved in a single major international multilateral troop operation in 2023. The new perspective was expressed in the government declaration of 2023: 'Sweden is now changing course in its overall foreign, security, and defence policy. The government will primarily pursue a Swedish and European foreign policy' (Billström 2023, authors' translation). The highest priority, as emphasised by the government and a nearly unanimous Riksdag (the Parliament of Sweden), was the imminent entry into NATO, with membership being formally obtained in March 2024.

Sweden's International Military Missions

Sweden has participated in more than 20 international missions led by either the UN, EU, or a combination of the UN/NATO since the end of the Cold War (Försvarsmakten 2023). The largest of these was the International Security Assistance Force (ISAF) in Afghanistan from 2002 to 2014, during which Sweden contributed nearly 8,000 men and women in uniform. However, Sweden has a longstanding tradition as an active participant in international military missions, and its peacekeeping efforts can be traced back to 1956.

Watching a border in a blue beret: The beginnings of Swedish peacekeeping

The first peacekeeping operation of the United Nations was initiated during the Suez Crisis in 1956. It primarily focused on observer roles, patrolling, and creating buffer zones, and operated under the principles outlined in Chapter 6 of the UN Charter. In the subsequent operations to come, small states like Sweden and Ireland that were not directly involved in the conflicts and not part of any military alliance often played a prominent role, as for example in the mission to Cyprus. However, the so-called Congo Crisis of 1960–1964 was the beginning of more complex missions that altered UN involvement in terms of including actual combat. The newly independent Republic of the Congo (now the Democratic Republic of the Congo) experienced a period of political upheaval and violence, which resulted in a UN deployment of peacekeeping forces to maintain stability and government support. However, the situation escalated into a full-scale civil war, involving various factions, regional conflicts, and international interests. Sweden participated by sending a contingent to Congo, comprising both army and air force personnel. Over the course of the four-year mission, more than 6,000 Swedish personnel served in Congo as part of the UN peacekeeping efforts. There were 19 deaths, an unprecedented number of casualties in Swedish peacekeeping missions (Tullberg 2012). After the Swedish mission in Congo, the Swedish UN operations returned to more traditional peacekeeping tasks in Cyprus and the Middle East until the end of the Cold War (Erikson Wolke 2019, 525–532).

After the Cold War: Three missions under NATO leadership

After 1991, Sweden expanded its participation in peacekeeping and crisis management efforts around the world. Starting in the latter half of 1990s, the officially nonaligned Sweden frequently contributed to NATO-led missions. The most extensive of these were the interventions in Bosnia and Herzegovina, Kosovo, and Afghanistan.

In August 1993, the Swedish government officially sanctioned the decision to contribute 800 soldiers to the United Nations, with an initial deployment to Tuzla in north-eastern Bosnia. The context for this mission was the ongoing conflict in the region, characterised by brutal ethnic cleansing carried out by Yugoslav and Bosnian Serb military forces. The primary objective of the UN deployment was to participate in operations with the goal of protecting refugees and aid convoys, establish safe zones, and to protect vulnerable communities (Ericson Wolke 2019, 532–533). Some contributing countries, such as Sweden, utilised the mandate under Chapter 7 of the UN Charter. This allowed for a more enforcement-oriented strategy, enabling the UN troops to use force more extensively to protect the civilian population (Henriksson 2023). Initially, the operation was carried out as a rather uncoordinated UN mission (UNPROFOR) with up to 39,000 personnel from approximately 40 countries. The failure of UNPROFOR to prevent the massacre in Srebrenica, where an estimated 8,000 Muslim men and boys were systematically killed, and the escalating violence, led to a more powerful international intervention. NATO launched an extensive air bombing campaign against Bosnian Serb military positions in August and September 1995. The objective was to halt the aggression and create conditions for negotiations, which led to the Dayton Agreement in December 1995. As a result of this agreement, UNPROFOR was replaced by the Implementation Force (IFOR), which was a NATO-led multinational peacekeeping force. This was the first time Swedish forces acted under the NATO flag (Ericson Wolke 2017, 533–534; Rapport från Riksdagen 2022, 30–33).

In the late 1990s, the conflict between predominantly Serb Yugoslav security forces and Kosovo-Albanian UCK guerrillas in Kosovo led to a significant humanitarian crisis. The conflict escalated into large-scale ethnic cleansing, with reports of widespread violence and expulsion of Kosovo's Albanian population by Serbian forces. NATO launched a military campaign against Serbian positions in March 1999, and the air and missile attacks targeted both military and strategic infrastructure in the province of Kosovo and the rest of the Federal Republic of Yugoslavia, including the capital city of Belgrade. Prior to the bombing campaign, in February 1999, the Swedish government approached NATO expressing Sweden's interest in participating in an international peacekeeping force, as a continuation of the intervention in Bosnia and Herzegovina. In May, the government presented a proposition to the Swedish Parliament regarding a Swedish troop contribution in Kosovo. The tasks of the Swedish KFOR battalion, consisting of over 800 personnel (the entire KFOR force led by NATO comprised 50,000 personnel), ranged from traditional peacekeeping duties to purely military combat tasks. The specific

Swedish mission was to prevent a Yugoslav attempt to retake the province by force, allowing NATO forces on the ground and in the air to keep Yugoslav forces outside Kosovo's borders. In June 2004, the Swedish troop contribution in Kosovo was reduced and continued to decrease until its conclusion in 2014 (Ericson Wolke 535–538).

Within a month after the terrorist attacks in New York and Washington on 11 September 2001, American bombers began to attack Afghan territory in pursuit of al-Qaeda operatives and to overthrow the Taliban government (Sjöstedt and Noreen 2021, 324). Many Western countries, apart from non-aligned ones like Sweden, began preparations for intervention in Afghanistan as part of the US-led Operation Enduring Freedom (OEF). However, Sweden was later invited to participate in a British-led multinational force in Afghanistan. The mission was guided by the framework of UN Security Council Resolution 1386, adopted in December 2001, establishing the International Security Assistance Force (ISAF) with the purpose of maintaining security and stability in Afghanistan. By 2003, ISAF was under NATO command. The Swedish government quickly responded by tasking its armed forces to prepare for the mission. Initially, the Swedish government proposed sending small contingents of 45 soldiers to serve within the British-led multinational force. Their main role focused on intelligence work and reconnaissance (Noreen *et al* 2017, 152–153).

By the end of 2004, the mission in Afghanistan underwent a radical change. The Swedish government tasked its armed forces to plan and prepare to assume command of a regional unit in Mazar-e-Sharif, Afghanistan's second-largest city. As one of a few non-NATO members, Sweden assumed the responsibility to lead one Provincial Reconstruction Team area (PRT) – out of a total of 26 PRTs located across Afghanistan – a decision that was welcomed by NATO and other troop-contributing states. The situation in the north, where Mazar-e-Sharif is located, was relatively calm compared to the south. However, a deteriorating security situation also affected the Swedish contingent and led to the first significant personnel losses in Swedish missions since the one in Congo in the 1960s. In response to the worsening conditions and the need for a stronger presence, the newly elected government decided in 2006 to expand the Swedish contingent to a maximum of 600 soldiers per rotation, each lasting six months (Sjöstedt and Noreen 2021, 326). Starting in 2012, the Swedish military mission, along with other participating nations, was tasked with providing support and training to the Afghan security forces during a transition process. Despite these efforts, the Taliban insurgency persisted and gained strength over the years – and its forces ultimately seized control of Afghanistan in 2021 following the withdrawal of foreign troops.

From Pragmatic Neutrality to Alliance Membership

Sweden has a long-standing tradition of neutrality in international affairs, but it is important to note that Swedish neutrality has never been absolute and has held various exceptions over time. Swedish neutrality gradually emerged during the nineteenth century as a widely adopted policy for small states to avoid getting involved in the conflicts of major powers. By remaining neutral, Sweden could stay out of conflict, and instead wait for an outcome without any risk of being caught in the middle (Wahlbäck 1984).

Swedish neutrality policy takes shape

One could argue that Swedish neutrality, as it was originally established in the nineteenth century and tested during the two World Wars, by no means corresponds with principles of international law. To the contrary, it was driven by national self-interest, aiming to avoid conflict at any cost through the strategy of evading military threats. During World War One, Sweden pledged to a policy that came to favour Germany (af Malmborg 2001, 201–202). This strategy became even more evident during World War Two when Sweden reached an agreement with Germany regarding transit traffic through Sweden. In practice, this meant that the policy of neutrality was abandoned on 8 July 1940, something which was recognized by Prime Minister Per Albin Hansson. After the cabinet meeting taking the decision of allowing German transit across Swedish territory, he pondered the idea that he had contributed to the abandonment of the neutrality policy. However, the message to the public was very different. Although the transit agreement meant that Sweden provided significant assistance to one of the warring parties, it was officially announced as merely a technical traffic matter. The implications for neutrality were not disclosed publicly as it was believed to have grave implications on Swedish public opinion (Dalsjö 2010a, 206–210; Johansson 1985).

The Cold War dual approach

Following the failed negotiations to form a Scandinavian defence alliance in 1949 – which resulted in Norway, Denmark, and later Iceland joining NATO – Sweden focused on developing its official policy of neutrality. Instead of isolating itself like other neutral states such as Switzerland, the ambition was rather to act as a bridge-builder between the East and the West, maintaining active diplomacy and fostering cooperation with both sides of the Cold War divide. However, while officially neutral, Sweden nevertheless pursued a confidential defence cooperation with NATO, as well as bilateral collaborations with the United States and the United Kingdom. These collaborations involved intelligence-sharing, joint military exercises, and the exchange of defence technologies. The activities were conducted discreetly, highlighting a 'dual approach' of maintaining active neutrality while engaging in confidential defence cooperation. This allowed the country to balance its security needs with a desire to remain independent, and avoid direct entanglements in the Cold War (Holmström 2023, 22–36).

Despite the fact the proposed Scandinavian Defence Union never materialised, the idea lived on in the form of informal agreements between the defence staff of Sweden, Norway, and Denmark, aiming to ensure coordinated Scandinavian actions in the event of war. They prepared joint operations, established personal contacts that could be utilised during wartime, coordinated planning, and attended each other's war colleges. This was intensely scrutinised when archives were opened at the end of the Cold War. Researchers and journalists showed no mercy in their critique of the contradictory standards of Swedish security policy. Wilhelm Agrell, the doyen of Swedish contemporary military history, was among the first to raise concerns. In his 1991 book *Den Stora Lögnen* (*The Great Lie*, authors' translation), Agrell highlighted what he believed to be a significant deception, or falsehood, in the official discourse of Swedish security policy.

Following Agrell's initial findings, a public commission was established to further investigate and shed light on facts from the first decades after World War Two. The commission aimed to uncover any hidden or undisclosed information that might have impacted Swedish security policy between 1949–1969. It eventually concluded that in the 1950s, US security officials had already declared that despite Sweden not being a formal member of NATO, Europe's defence would benefit from SAF being closely associated with, and cooperating with, its NATO neighbours and the United States. This stance was emphasised by US President Dwight Eisenhower in 1960 when he adopted the policy of assurance of US military assistance to Sweden, should it ever be attacked by the Soviet Union. The United States was also to 'encourage other NATO countries (such as Denmark and Norway) to maintain discreet contacts with SAF as a basis for possible future active military cooperation' (SOU 1994, 11; 13, authors' translation). Despite the Swedish government being aware of these plans, Prime Minister Tage Erlander denied any such military collaboration when the issue was debated in the Riksdag. Such secrecy and double standards *vis-à-vis* the public was a recurring pattern throughout the Cold War. The unofficial cooperation continued for decades, and in the 1980s Sweden was seen by one of the American ambassadors to NATO as the 'seventeenth member of NATO' (Holmström 2023, 32).

After the Cold War: As close to NATO as possible

Through various covert interactions, different Swedish governments, both conservative and social democratic, laid the groundwork for a more open collaboration with NATO when the Cold War ended. A more general background for such collaborations is found in the critical changes of the geopolitical environment in Europe in the early 1990s. After the end of the Cold War and the dissolution of the Soviet Union, the Eastern Bloc and the Warsaw Pact ceased to exist as a unified counterforce to NATO – thus eliminating the traditional adversarial relationship between the two blocs. Within this context, the Social Democratic government submitted a 'non–binding statement of intent' to NATO, expressing Sweden's interest in participating in an international peacekeeping force in Kosovo (Ericson Wolke 2019, 536). According to such a request, Swedish troops would operate within a NATO-led force for the second time. Previously, a Swedish force had served under NATO command in Bosnia and Herzegovina (IFOR). Such an engagement would later be repeated within the framework of the NATO-led mission to Afghanistan.

The annual reports from SAF in the 2000s reveal that adaptation to NATO standards was regarded to be of the highest importance. For example, in a 2003 report it is highlighted that 'cooperation with NATO must be as close as Sweden's security policy line allows' (Försvarsmakten 2004). Still, from NATO's point of view, there was an explicit recognition of the Swedish military's non-alignment. A NATO evaluation, assessing Sweden as a partner country, clearly states that Sweden continues its close cooperation with NATO without compromising its position on freedom from military alliances (NATO 2013).

The first decade of the new millennium revealed an interesting paradox. Parallel to the de-prioritisation of Sweden's national defence – defence expenditures as a percentage of GDP decreased from 2.8 per cent in 1993 to 1.3 per cent in 2009 – Sweden increased its engagement in advanced international exercises, primarily with NATO forces. This engagement also occurred in real-life situations, such as in Libya in 2011, where Sweden conducted aerial reconnaissance with a small number of Gripen fighter jets. This occurred after the Swedish fighter jet divisions were reduced from 20 to four divisions (Holmström 2023, 589). As accurately depicted by Finnish President Sauli Niinistö, Sweden represented a 'military vacuum' in 2013 (Holmström 2023, 596). This vacuum, however, was only apparent in a Nordic security context. In the international arena, SAF – in collaboration with NATO primarily – developed in a manner that would have been unthinkable during the Cold War. A parliamentary evaluation of Sweden's participation in international military operations since the 1990s concluded that the experiences, especially from the NATO-led missions, 'are assessed to have significantly contributed to the professional development of officers and soldiers. Particularly those who have participated in actual combat situations' (Rapport från Riksdagen. 2022, 9, authors' translation). It is particularly emphasised that interoperability with other countries had developed. Additionally, Sweden's participation in international operations enabled the signing of a Memorandum of Understanding between Sweden and NATO. This agreement meant that

Sweden would more swiftly both provide and receive support from NATO in the event of a crisis or war (Rapport från Riksdagen 2022, 80).

Around 2010, Sweden's close cooperation with NATO and the United States began to face criticism, primarily from members of parliament belonging to the Left and the Green parties. These critics expressed concerns about Sweden's involvement in the ISAF mission in Afghanistan. The debates surrounding Sweden's role in ISAF were heated, and differing opinions emerged across the Swedish political landscape. The Left Party in particular, known for their non-alignment positions, were vocal in their opposition to Sweden's participation in the NATO-led mission. Even the Sweden Democrats, who had become a political force to be reckoned with, were outspoken opponents of participation in ISAF. Critics argued that Sweden's cooperation with NATO compromised its long-standing policy of neutrality and could potentially draw Sweden into conflicts that were not directly related to its national interests (Sjöstedt and Noreen 2021).

A key area of discontent concerned whether the Swedish military engagement in Afghanistan was a war-fighting operation or a peace and development mission. This topic continued to resurface throughout the duration of the ISAF operation and was often brought up in parliamentary debates. The Left Party described the Swedish contribution in terms of war, while those who supported the Swedish mission downplayed this image. The Swedish government tried to tone down the combat activities to gain broad parliamentary support for the continued participation in ISAF. Instead, the humanitarian efforts undertaken by Swedish forces were emphasised. The overall idea that Sweden was an international humanitarian actor to be reckoned with, highly appreciated by other states and actors, eventually pleased even the most critical voices against military engagement. This view created a form of 'catch-all-identity', or in other words, Sweden was both a significant security actor, contributing to international security, and a recognized humanitarian entrepreneur, working for justice, equality, democracy, and human rights (Noreen, Sjöstedt and Ångström 2017, 156).

After the finalisation of ISAF, details about the Swedish mission and its level of combat involvement were divulged. A public inquiry confirmed that the Swedish contingents had increasingly become involved in combat incidents, aligning with the Counterinsurgency (COIN) concept (SOU 2017, 75, 85–86). This highlights the complexity of the Swedish government's portrayal of the Swedish participation in ISAF and the difficulties in attempting to reconcile different perspectives. Firstly, the government and other political supporters of the ISAF mission strived to emphasise Sweden's commitment to peacekeeping, making its involvement consistent with its 'peace nation' tradition. This framing was primarily directed towards opposition parties and the public in order to gain their support and maintain a positive perception of the Swedish participation. In contrast, the reality was that Swedish troops were involved in combat in Afghanistan, although this was not divulged to the public until the mission had ended (Sjöstedt and Noreen 2021, 334–336).

From being NATO's '17th member' to a member-candidate

Following the conclusion of the ISAF mission and Russia's annexation of Crimea in 2014, Sweden experienced a notable shift in its defence priorities. In 2015, Sweden allocated only 1.1 per cent of its GDP to defence expenditures. However, in 2016, a parliamentary decision was made to expand defence costs for the first time since the Cold War. This decision included the protection of Gotland, a strategically significant island in the Baltic Sea. As a result, military spending was set to double between 2016 and 2025, indicating a significant increase in resources allocated (Holmström 2023, 602–603). Despite the increased resources to strengthen SAF and national defence, a clear line continued to be drawn regarding NATO membership which was considered inappropriate for several reasons: Swedish membership in NATO was deemed to increase tensions in Northern Europe, and the Swedish political discourse continuously emphasised that non-alignment 'serves Sweden well and contributes to stability and security in Northern Europe' (Wieslander 2021, 36). Additionally, public opinion was not considered ready for Swedish membership in NATO. Between 2014 and 2021 the proportion of Swedish people in favour of membership hovered at around 30 per cent, and among supporters of the ruling Social Democratic Party, the proportion was only around 20 per cent (Bjereld and Oscarsson 2023, 8).

This dual act of, on the one hand, close cooperation with NATO countries to the extent possible – and, on the other hand, a steadfast rejection of NATO membership, was the official Swedish line from 2014 to spring 2022. This strategy is commonly referred to as the Hultqvist Doctrine, after then-Minister of Defence, Peter Hultqvist (Wieslander 2021). On 13 May 2022, the Hultqvist Doctrine ended abruptly when a parliamentary task force, which included Hultqvist, presented the report 'A deteriorating security policy situation – consequences for Sweden'. The report concluded that given the security situation, NATO membership was the way ahead. Two days later, the governing Social Democratic Party, backed by broad parliamentary consensus, made the decision that Sweden would apply for membership in NATO (Bjereld 2023, 18). What caused this sharp U-turn by the Social Democrats? The simple answer would be Russia's invasion of Ukraine on 24 February 2022, a day which changed the European security order. However, the Swedish government continued to adhere to the Hultqvist Doctrine after the invasion. On 8 March, Prime Minister Magdalena Anderson had condemned the invasion in strong terms and firmly maintained that Swedish membership in NATO was out of the question: 'In this situation, a Swedish NATO application would further destabilise the situation in Europe' (Andersson in Bjereld 2023, 17).

Russian aggression was obviously an important background factor for Sweden's NATO shift. Nevertheless, it took one and a half months after the Russian invasion of Ukraine for the Swedish government to take a clear public stance in favour of membership. The actions of neighbouring Finland can help explain why Sweden changed its course (Bjereld 2023). Finland's situation, with its long border with Russia, has always been a crucial factor in Swedish security assessments. Finland's sensitive relationship with the Soviet Union after World War Two is viewed as a key reason as to why Sweden in the late 1940s could neither consider joining NATO, nor participate in a westward-oriented Scandinavian defence alliance (Dalsjö 2010a, 216). The end of the Cold War put an end to this delicate situation, making Finland and Sweden equally eager to solidify a good relationship with NATO. Russia's invasion of Ukraine became both a wake-up call and a window of opportunity for the Finnish government to take the next step. Assessing the increased threat level due to its proximity to an aggressive and neighbouring great power, the Finnish government was quicker and more explicit than Sweden in stating an interest to reconsider its non-alignment policy. Although the details of the relationship and communication between Finland and Sweden during the spring of 2022 have yet to be revealed, it can be contended that Sweden desired to keep pace with Finland, which led to both countries jointly applying for NATO membership on 17 and 18 May 2022 respectively (Bjereld 2023, 17–24).

Concluding remarks

Sweden advocated a non-aligned foreign policy aimed at neutrality in war. This principle had materialised in the form of a dogma or doctrine that has been proclaimed in foreign policy statements since 1945, regardless of which political party held power. However, political and military leadership alike actively pursued military cooperation with NATO, especially the Nordic NATO countries, the United Kingdom, and the United States – while the Swedish public was kept in the dark on this matter. Swedish official doctrine can nonetheless be viewed as a clever strategy. The numerous statements regarding how non-alignment was a policy that served Sweden well clearly resonated with the public. The doctrine also served to fend off possible criticism from the political opposition for 70 years, except for a few debates in the 1950s, and the above-mentioned critiques against the involvement in ISAF. Furthermore, it also served to construct Sweden as an independent non-aligned country that could equally criticize American bombings of North Vietnam during the Vietnam War and the Soviet invasion of Afghanistan. The doctrine helped Sweden to gain international recognition as a 'peace nation' and a 'do-gooder' in international affairs (Sjöstedt and Noreen 2021). The question remains, however, to what extent this dual approach can be viewed as morally just. For decades, the general public was kept in the dark regarding the extent to which the military cooperation and support, clearly contrasting the policy of neutrality, were institutionalized practices. Also in the post-Cold War context, the interaction between Sweden and NATO has been a much more close-knit enterprise than would be expected in a relationship between an alliance and a non-aligned state. Thus, although Sweden's membership application to NATO travelled along a somewhat bumpy road, the transition from being the unofficial '17th member' to now being official the 32nd will likely be a smooth one.

References

Agrell, Willhelm. 1991. *Den stora lögnen: ett säkerhetspolitiskt dubbelspel i alltför många akter.* Stockholm: Ordfronts förlag.

Billström, Tobias. 2023. Utrikesdeklarationen   [Foreign Policy Declaration for the Swedish Parliament] 15 February. Stockholm: The Swedish Government, https://www.regeringen.se/tal/2023/022/utrikesdeklarationen-2023

Bjereld, Ulf. 1995. "Critic or Mediator - Sweden in World-Politics, 1945–90". *Journal of Peace Research* 32, no 1, 23–35.

Bjereld, Ulf & Henrik Oscarsson. 2023. "Jordskred i svensk NATO-opinion efter Rysslands invasion av Ukraina." In *Ovisshetens tid*, edited by Andersson, Ulrika, Patrik Öhberg, Johan Martinsson & Nora Theorin. Göteborg: SOM-insitutet, Göteborgs universitet.

Bjereld, Ulf. 2023. "It's NOT the Security, Stupid! Sweden's Decision to Apply for Membership in NATO". Paper for presentation at the ISA 2023 Annual Convention, 15–18 March. Montreal Canada.

Dalsjö, Robert. 2010a. "Från Stormaktsspel till neutralitetspolitik: Några huvudlinjer i svensk säkerhetspolitik från 1700-tal till Sovjetväldets fall". In *Svensk säkerhetspolitik i Europa och världen*, edited by Kjell Engelbrekt & Jan Ångström, 203–237. Stockholm: Norstedts Juridik.

Dalsjö, Robert. 2010b. "Från neutralitet till solidaritet: Omgestaltningen av Sveriges säkerhetspolitik efter det kalla kriget". In *Svensk säkerhetspolitik i Europa och världen*, edited by Kjell Engelbrekt & Jan Ångström, 61–80. Stockholm: Norstedts Juridik.

Ericson Wolke, Lars. 2019. "Fredsbevarande eller fredsframtvingande? Svenskt deltagande i internationella truppinsatser 1921–2017". *Historisk Tidskrift* 39, no 3, 511–552.

Försvarsmakten. 2004. Årsrapport från perspektivplaneringen 2002–2003. Målbildsinriktningar inför försvarsbeslutet 2004, Rapport 7. Stockholm: Försvarmakten. [Yearly Report from Perspective Planning 2002–2003. Target Structures for the Defence Decision 2004].

Försvarsmakten, 2023. Försvarsmakten utomlands. [The Swedish Armed Forces missions abroad]:
https://www.forsvarsmakten.se/sv/var-verksamhet/forsvarsmakten-utomlands/pagaende-internationella-insatser/
https://www.forsvarsmakten.se/sv/var-verksamhet/forsvarsmakten-utomlands/avslutade-internationella-insatser/
https://www.forsvarsmakten.se/sv/information-och-fakta/var-historia/mer-historia/avslutade-truppinsatser/

Henriksson, Ulf. 2023. Interview by Martin Wicklin, 28 April 2023. Stockholm: Swedish Radio.https://sverigesradio.se/avsnitt/ulf-henricsson-sheriffen-som-stoppade-en-massaker-i-bosnien

Holmström, Mikael. 2023. *Den dolda alliansen. Sveriges hemliga NATO-förbindelser*. Stockholm: Natur & Kultur.

Johansson, Alf W. 1985. *Per Albin och kriget: samlingsregeringen och utrikespolitiken under andra världskriget*. Stockholm: Tiden.

Löfven, Stefan. 2017. Regeringsförklaringen [Government Declaration] 12 September 2017. Stockholm: The Swedish Government.
https://www.regeringen.se/tal/2017/09/regeringsforklaringen-den-12-september-2017/

af Malmborg, Mikael. 2001. *Neutrality and State-building in Sweden*. Houndsmills: Palgrave

Ministry for Foreign Affairs. 1992. Documents on Swedish Foreign Policy 1992. New Series 1: C 41 Stockholm: Ministry for Foreign Affairs.

NATO. 2013. 'Planning and Review Process'. Available at Stockholm: Försvarsdepartementet. http://www.regeringen.se/sveriges-regering/forsvarsdepartementet/

Noreen, Erik, Roxanna Sjöstedt & Jan Ångström. 2017. "Why small states join big wars: the case of Sweden in Afghanistan 2002–2014". *International Relations.* 31, no 2, 145–168.

Rapport från Riksdagen. 2022. Sveriges deltagande i fem internationell militära insatser—en uppföljning av konsekvenserna för den nationella försvarsförmågan. 2021/22. RFR 13. Stockholm: Sveriges Riksdag https://www.riksdagen.se/sv/dokument-och-lagar/dokument/rapport-fran-riksdagen/sveriges-deltagande-i-fem-internationella-militara_h90wrfr13/

Sjöstedt, Roxanna & Erik Noreen. 2021. "When peace nations go to war: Examining the narrative transformation of Sweden and Norway in Afghanistan". *European Journal of International Security.* 6, 318–337.

SOU 1994:11. Om kriget kommit … – Förberedelser för mottagande av militärt bistånd 1949–1969. Stockholm: Sveriges Riksdag.

SOU 2017:6. Sverige i Afghanistan 2002–2014. Betänkande av Afghanistanutredningen. Stockholm: Sveriges Riksdag.

Tullberg, Andreas. 2012. *"We are in the Congo now" Sweden and the trinity of peacekeeping during the Congo crisis 1960–1964.* Lund: Lund University

Wahlbäck, Krister. 1984. *Den svenska neutralitetens rötter.* Stockholm; Utrikesdepartementet.

Wieslander. Anna 2021. "'The Hultqvist doctrine': Swedish Security and defence policy after the Russian annexation of Crimea". *Defence Studies* 22 no 1, 35–39.

3

From Cold War 'Neutrality' to the West: Finland's Route to the European Union and NATO

JUSSI PAKKASVIRTA AND HANNA TUOMINEN

The meaning of neutrality is contested and has been used in various ways in different historical and political contexts. Originally, neutrality was interpreted as a legal term, referring to a state's non-participation in a war between other states. In the post-1945 period, it was superseded by a more political notion of neutrality as non-participation and impartiality in international conflicts in general, and East-West conflict in particular (Hakovirta 1988, 8). Instead of non-participation in conflicts, it came to refer to non-participation in military alliances. Hence, the Cold War framework modified the concept, and it received new meaning as a foreign policy orientation in peacetime. These orientations were the result of different compromises, and consequently there were various models of neutrality. Amidst this, the Finnish interpretation of neutrality is unique and nuanced, and comprehending the difference between the political and military dimension of Finland's neutrality helps to understand the evolving Finnish position.

Neutrality can be a temporary or permanent foreign policy choice. States may voluntarily choose to be neutral or be coerced by other states to remain neutral. In the Finnish case, the policy of neutrality is closely related to the Treaty of Friendship, Cooperation and Mutual Assistance (FCMA) with the Soviet Union, forming the basis for their bilateral relations between 1948–1992. This created a peculiar tradition to combine the FCMA and neutrality: On the one hand, neutrality was represented as a virtue – but, on the other hand, it was promoted out of necessity (see Rainio-Niemi 2021). Finland pursued a policy of neutrality to maintain its independence and avoided being drawn into conflicts between the Eastern and Western blocs. Through skillful diplomacy and social welfare policies, Finland managed to become a member of the Nordic Council

(1955) and build firm relations with the West. However, Finnish neutrality was particularly vulnerable and dubious in the eyes of both blocs.

After the end of the Cold War and the dissolution of the Soviet Union, the Finnish position changed dramatically – even if Finland continued to stay outside of military alliances. In 1995, Finnish membership in the European Union officially ended its self-defined neutrality and was replaced by a strong commitment to military non-alignment. Since 1995, government reports on foreign, security, and defence policy have underlined the relevance of EU membership and military non-alignment – even though Finland has developed close partnership and interoperability with NATO and participated in various forms of international military cooperation and crisis management tasks. Finland has also continuously evaluated the changes in its security environment and consequences of military alignment through reports and studies, and a NATO-option has been maintained in government programs.

In 2022, because of the Russian invasion of Ukraine, Finland rapidly reassessed its security situation (Finnish Government, 2022) and applied for NATO membership. Joining NATO in April 2023 finally abolished the long-term practice of military non-alignment. Even if Finland no longer officially followed a policy of neutrality, key foreign policy documents continued to emphasise Nordic cooperation and its extant profile in international relations – once key elements of Finland's Cold War neutrality policy in line with other countries such as Sweden. The preference for neutrality and independence is especially relevant because of the preferred high international profile of the Nordics in crisis management, peace mediation and humanitarian aid (Wivel 2017, 490). This emphasises the evolving interpretation of neutrality as a norm and both continuity and change in the Finnish positioning.

In this chapter, we will first discuss how neutrality can be approached from different theoretical perspectives, and we frame Finnish policy in this respect. Secondly, we look at the Finnish case and its background by acknowledging and discussing the structural, external, and domestic factors shaping its position as a neutral state. After that, we briefly discuss Finnish history, and analyse how the end of the Cold War and decision to join the EU fundamentally shook the foundations of the Finnish policy of neutrality. Finally, we reflect upon how the slow development towards NATO membership has pushed down the key elements associated with neutrality.

Different explanations for neutrality

Different theoretical approaches to neutrality may explain the decisions made by policymakers at different historical moments. These theories tend to outline rather pure, ideal, concepts whilst the picture is much blurrier in actual politics. The preconditions for adopting neutrality also vary from state to state, which makes it difficult to suggest any general explanations. However, realist, liberal and constructivist approaches can help to position the Finnish policy of neutrality in the wider European framework and explain foreign and security policy options and preferences at different times.

Realist explanations underline the influence of structural factors and external environment in the positions of states. During the Cold War, several European states – such as Finland and Sweden – adopted a neutral position as they were located between the two opposing blocs. However, the perceptions and misperceptions of others, mainly conflicting powers, influenced evaluations of neutrality (Hakovirta 1988, 32). As the states were located between the two blocs, their neutrality was 'suspicious' and both blocs found it difficult to fully trust the position. For example, the Soviet Union accepted Finnish neutrality without reservation only in 1989 (Aunesluoma and Rainio-Niemi 2016, 56). This reflected the obvious tensions between the policy of neutrality and the FCMA treaty. For the Western bloc, Finnish neutrality was particularly vague because of this same treaty. Internationally, Finland also refrained from publicly criticising the Soviet Union (Forsberg 2018; Möttölä 2021). For example, it abstained from the non-binding UN General Assembly resolutions concerning conflicts in Hungary (1956), Czechoslovakia (1968) and Afghanistan (1979).

The liberal position adopts a rather different focus as it underlines the importance of international law, multilaterally negotiated norms, shared values and principles. These provide instruments for small states to balance great powers and compensate for their own weaknesses. Importantly, close cooperation and support for international organisations such as the Council of Europe (CoE), the United Nations (UN) and the Organization for Security and Cooperation in Europe (OSCE) formed a beneficial strategy for small states. All the Nordic states have traditionally been keen supporters of these organisations and active advocates of associated norms. Instead of the military, strategic and economic aspects underlined by realists, the liberal position acknowledges the key role of values such as human rights, democracy and rule of law, and emphasises the interdependence of actors. These values are considered to strengthen the prospects of a peaceful order and lead to wider cooperation between states.

Liberalism acknowledges various domestic factors and decision-making levels influencing the foreign policy of states. Here, of course, opinions may be divided between parties, key decision-makers and even between the elites and public. On the one hand, for Finland the association with a Western worldview, liberal norms and values was important during the Cold War. On the other hand, neutrality was an important norm shaping the expected and appropriate behaviour of Finland's balancing between the blocs. Domestically, the 'neutrality doctrine' enjoyed wide acceptance among the public and policymakers (Aunesluoma and Rainio-Niemi 2016, 60). Many Finns still consider it as a success story of Finnish policy during the Cold War (Forsberg 2018). However, in the current understanding, norms are treated as flexible, constantly developing entities. In this respect, the understanding and interpretations of the neutrality norm may also evolve, which leads us to constructivism.

As neutrality is closely associated with state identity (Aunesluoma and Rainio-Niemi 2016; Forsberg 2016), in constructivist approaches, identities shape states' interests and understanding of appropriateness. Structures and external factors matter, but actors may interpret them differently. There are both collective and individual identity narratives, which can be used politically. Policymakers and the public may promote several competing domestic identity narratives, leading to different lines of action. Political decision-makers have the freedom to choose which identities, or emphases, they use to justify specific policies (Forsberg 2016, 365). However, even similar identities can be used to rationalise contrasting policy options which makes identity a challenging concept to analyse.

Identity-based arguments are often influential in policy debates as they appeal to emotions and sense of community (Forsberg 2016, 365). Emphasising differences between 'us' and 'them' is one effective strategy showing how identities are used in policymaking. This leads to the construction of in- and out-groups to identify with. For Finland the essential background community was the Nordic group. During the Cold War, the peace-loving and rational Nordics aimed to differentiate themselves from conflict-prone Europe (Browning 2008, 27). The region, especially Sweden and Finland, represented themselves as non-aligned neutrals, as a third way and alternative between the capitalist West and the communist East (Wivel 2017, 492). However, there has always been a slight difference between Finnish and Swedish neutrality. The Swedish version is more normative and identity based, while the Finnish version relates more to strategic security interests and political (or realist) practice. Interestingly, Lödén claims that countries with comparatively limited identity-based neutrality would leave their non-aligned position sooner than those with much invested in identity. This point suggests that Finland might be more prepared to change its position regarding NATO membership than Sweden (Lödén 2012, 277). This is exactly what happened in 2022 when Finland rapidly changed its attitude towards NATO membership.

Realist explanations seem predominant in the case of small states such as Finland. Small states are considered weak, and they have no resources to resist great powers. Hence, they either join alliances or proclaim neutrality to survive. Finnish self-identity outlined in political speeches and documents underline its status as a small state. Smallness is also used to rationalise previous non-alignment policy (Forsberg 2016, 365). Yet, realists are less capable of explaining why neutrality would be the first option for small states instead of joining alliances (Lödén 2012). Geopolitical reasons are used to explain this choice – as for Finland and Austria, the need to adopt a policy of neutrality came from outside. As Rainio-Niemi (2021) notes, this represented neutrality as a compromise. The options of small states are limited, and often the main task for neutrals has been to convince others that they don't have any hostile military intentions, while simultaneously wanting to be militarily strong.

Structures and agency in shaping neutrality

According to Lödén (2012), it is important to acknowledge both internal and external factors that shape the foreign and security policies of neutrals. The small state status has prioritised realist explanations and the need to adapt to external changes. Mainly this refers to how Russia has developed, and what kind of security threats this development has caused. Furthermore, realist interpretations have been visible in discussions on Finland's NATO membership. Finland is considered too small to defend itself alone, and the EU or Sweden do not provide enough security guarantees (Forsberg 2018). The US role and relevance in European security structures has therefore been predominant.

Secondly, Finland's relations to international institutions such as the Nordic Council, EU, NATO and the UN have been important factors shaping its preferences, as liberals assume. The UN especially became a key arena in which to demonstrate a distinctive policy line and to monitor the other neutrals' stances on international disputes. From the 1960s onward, neutrality was increasingly associated with an active foreign policy stance (Aunesluoma and Rainio-Niemi 2016, 56). The neutral states acted as mediators and bridge-builders in UN forums. The Nordic states occupied a privileged position and a reputation as promoters of international peace and security (Wivel 2017). This can be seen, for example, via Finland's contribution to the UN's peacekeeping troops – like the other Nordics. Later, it developed mediation capabilities, analytical expertise and other 'good services' in the UN (Möttölä 2021, 219).

The Nordic states have had highly diverse institutional relations and have made their own distinct choices in foreign and security policy (Brommesson et al. 2023). In the Finnish case, the Nordic dimension has been preferred but has always been more reserved due to immediate security concerns (Ojanen and Raunio 2018). After the Cold War, the institutional arrangements and state priorities changed. The role of the UN was questioned and the importance of NATO and the EU and several other more informal organisations increased.

The Nordic approach became an integral part of the European/EU/Western approach, rendering a unique progressive model less visible (Wivel 2017). Due to Russian aggressiveness, there was also a convergence of Nordic threat perceptions and foreign and security policy choices (Brommesson et al. 2023).

Thirdly, changes in the security, economic and normative structures have shaped the potential of neutrality. As the Cold War ended, the neutral countries lost the need to promote neutrality as it wasn't necessary any longer. However, Finland's geopolitical location meant that security concerns remained essential. Maintaining strong territorial defence and conscription were uniquely Finnish features. The collapse of the Soviet Union had extreme effects on Finnish foreign trade, and the early 1990s saw one of the worst economic crises in Finland's history. European economic integration provided better possibilities to prosper. In that context, it was no longer necessary to build national identity around neutrality because European integration gave a better frame. It was normatively attractive for neutral Finland, Sweden and Austria. Furthermore, issues such as transnational immigration, environmental and economical threats had to be dealt with at a higher level (Agius 2011, 371). The influence of European states on each other's policies, horizontal Europeanization, strengthened common European values and collective identity.

Hence, despite the relevance of structural factors, state agency is reflected in the manner policymakers and wider society react to external realities. The constructivist approach emphasises the interaction between structural and agential factors. As reality is socially constructed, much depends on how the structural factors are interpreted and how actors react via their own agency to changing circumstances. During the Cold War, the idea of neutrality became deeply internalised in the minds of Finnish policymakers and the wider public, and an essential part of the Finnish national identity. However, as the Cold war ended, the dramatic structural change was not as strongly reflected in Finnish agency as was perhaps expected. There was still much continuity with the traditional neutrality policy, even if the adopted non-alignment policy excluded political neutrality. According to Forsberg, knowledge of psychological factors, domestic politics and national identity discourses gives essential insights into understanding Finnish post-Cold War policy and its relationship to NATO. As he demonstrates, the different views of political leaders and parties, as well as the general public, can be used to explain why Finland did not join NATO directly after the end of the Cold War – and instead preferred Finland's unique 'NATO-option' – to maintain domestic consensus (Forsberg 2018).

Even if many political leaders have emphasised cooperation as well as prudence and stability in the adopted policies, the potential for change has been maintained. Neutrality and non-alignment have been considered options maximising Finland's freedom of choice. When circumstances change, Finland can change its position as both its EU and NATO memberships have demonstrated. A supporting internal factor for rapid decision-making is Finland's consensus-oriented domestic political culture, especially in foreign and security policy. This orientation, and trust in political leadership, can be traced to the historical experiences and Finnish claims of neutrality (Aunesluoma and Rainio-Niemi 2016, 62).

Cold War Finland and Active Neutrality

In historical terms, the bedrock of Finland's security policy line seemed clear and unchanging. Neutrality has been useful in various periods, in different ways. Here we can differentiate clearly between external and internal factors. In short, Finnish foreign and security policy has been defined around three pillars: 1) Finland's relations with the USSR/Russia, 2) Finland's own defence ability and sovereignty, and 3) Finland's relationship with the West, including the neighbouring Nordic countries. If one pillar breaks, it must be compensated by another. Finland's route to neutrality – and from neutrality – has brought these pillars out clearly. When the Russian Empire collapsed in 1917, Finland became independent and looked first at the Baltic defence politics for ten years, and adopted neutrality. During 1939–1944, Finland's defence ability was challenged heavily, but relations with the Soviet Union were managed. During the Cold War, relations with the West and the other Nordics were developed step by step. After the Cold War, all pillars were maintained in some balance. In 2014, and especially in 2022, when Russia started its full-scale attack on Ukraine, the Russian pillar ceased to exist. Now, Finland does not opt for neutrality and its value seems quite weak for the foreseeable future.

Stories of violence and images of threats based on relations between Finland and the 'other' have always played a role in Finnish national narratives. This highlights the identity-based interpretation of history. Especially since the October Revolution in 1917, Soviet Russia has been the other in the strengthening of Finnish national identity. The Finnish declaration of independence in December 1917 was followed by a brutal civil war (1917–1918) between the reds (socialist workers and landless peasants) and whites (the bourgeoisie and landowners) who won the war. While the official and strongly anti-socialist 'white state' equated Russians with communists, many old negative stereotypes of Russia and Russians strengthened in a new ideological way, and relations between the two nations remained tense (Nortio et. al. 2022). During the interwar period, Soviet Russia was naturally perceived as an existential threat since the key leaders of the 'reds' had escaped there, and it was widely believed that external assistance was needed to counterbalance Soviet power (Forsberg 2018).

At the beginning of World War Two, Nordic countries declared their neutrality but only Sweden was saved from being drawn into the war. In November 1939, the Soviet Union attacked Finland, soon after Stalin and Hitler agreed to a pact dividing up the neighbouring borderlands (the Molotov-Ribbentrop pact and its secret protocol). During the war, Finland first fought a separate Winter War against the Soviet Union, followed by a Continuation War as a co-belligerent with Germany. During the wars, the Finns suffered 90,000 casualties and killed an even larger number of Soviets (320,000). In the peace treaty of 1944, Finland lost more than 10 per cent of its pre-war territory, including the major city Vyborg, to the Soviet Union. Finnish neutrality was essentially different from Austria, Sweden and Switzerland. Finland balanced between two tracks – its Eastern policy and policy of neutrality. Hence, the space of Finnish neutrality also varied in the Cold War tensions, and Finland needed the capability to adapt to ongoing crises. To the contrary, neutral Sweden was actively condemning both superpowers in international crises while Finland avoided such criticism (Forsberg and Vaahtoranta 2001, 70). Neutrality for Sweden was a prerequisite for a high profile in foreign policy (Lödén 2012).

Finnish neutrality after the Second World War, and especially since the 1960s, has been called 'active neutrality'. This is a foreign policy concept built under the leadership of President Urho Kekkonen, who tried to open more margins for action, developing his predecessor Juho Kusti Paasikivi's more cautious neutrality after World War Two. The idea of active neutrality was to retain Finnish independence while maintaining good relations and trade with members of both NATO and the Warsaw Pact. The Paasikivi-Kekkonen doctrine emphasised the geographical facts, pragmatic relations and good communication with the Soviet Union – seeking for the peaceful coexistence of capitalist and socialist countries. This has later been connected to the notion of 'Finlandisation', a concept referring to the exceptionally problematic policy of neutrality in relations between Finland and Russia (e.g., Uutela 2020, Arter 2023). It has also been used more negatively to describe Finland as being heavily influenced by the Soviet Union during the Cold War (Moisio 2008).

It is of high, but often ignored, importance to understand the contextual relevance of the Nordic affinity and legacy in all its aspects for Finland's performance in the Cold War (Möttölä 2021, 215). The most visible success of the Finnish policy of active neutrality was the Conference on Security and Co-operation in Europe, organised in Helsinki in 1975. This high-level political meeting did not have the force of a treaty, but it added to the atmosphere of détente in the Cold War, recognized the boundaries of post-war Europe and established a mechanism for minimising political and military tensions between the East and the West whilst trying to improve human rights in the Socialist Bloc.

Active neutrality is credited by many, not only for its practical and successful trade policies, but also for its manner of creating security and stability in Finland and in Northern Europe. It permitted Finland's market economy to have advantageous bilateral trade with the Soviet Union and to keep pace with Western Europe. Active neutrality allowed Finland to also gradually take part in European integration. However, the discourse of active neutrality was also misused, especially during the 26 years of Kekkonen's presidency. His authoritarian style of mastering foreign relations deeply affected domestic politics as his omnipotent divide-and-rule attitude silenced political opposition. Consequently, inside Finland, active neutrality somewhat weakened democracy. Yet, it was a success story in creating a margin of action (Arter 2023).

The road to the European Union and Finnish post-neutrality

The Finnish debate on European Community (EC) in the 1990s was preceded by the decisions of the two other neutrals, Austria (1989) and Sweden (1990), to join the Union. Sweden's announcement came as a surprise for Finnish decision-makers who were not informed about it beforehand. This created anger, and even a crisis mentality, among the politicians. During the Cold War, Finland was eager to seek a similar international position with Sweden (Forsberg and Vaahtoranta 2001, 70) and saw their fates interrelated. Domestically, the political parties remained divided on the membership – and many parties had active and visible opponents in their rows. Interestingly, the critique included the argument that Finland would lose its own successful way of practising neutrality. Proclaimed neutrality also caused suspicions in the EU and the neutral states would need to show loyalty to the new Common Foreign and Security Policy (CFSP) by signing a declaration that they would fully accept its contents.

The new Finnish government of 1991, led by Prime Minister Esko Aho, adopted a more flexible attitude towards European integration. This was despite the disagreement on the issue within his own party, the Centre Party. The National Coalition, the Social Democrats and the Swedish People's Party first advocated for membership in 1991, and these integration-minded forces became more influential across society. In February 1992, President Mauno Koivisto announced the intention of the Finnish government to apply for EC/EU membership. However, opinion polls showed varying degrees of support for membership through 1990-94. In October 1994 when the consultative referendum was arranged, 57 per cent of voters accepted membership (Raunio and Tiilikainen 2003). In January 1995, Finland became a member of the EU, and was now politically aligned. The official Finnish view was that its neutrality ended at this moment.

The membership decision has been outlined in the literature as a complete reversal of foreign policy (Browning 2008) and re-identification (Raunio and Tiilikainen 2003, 11). Forsberg and Vaahtoranta (2001) and Agius (2011) use the term post-neutrality. However, the development has also been considered as a natural continuity from neutrality to the liberal West. The Finnish EU policy paradigm has many features from previous times – it has been described as pragmatic, cooperative and constructive. In the EU, Finland was more pro-integrationist and adaptive than Sweden or Denmark. Yet, as most of the EU member states were also members of the NATO, the non-alignment policy presented a dilemma. Finland and Sweden were concerned that they would not have an equal position with those member states belonging to NATO (Forsberg and Vaahtoranta 2001, 74).

In the mid-1990s, NATO announced its open-door policy – but as EU integration was prioritised, the NATO membership question was not seen as much in the Finnish debate. In post-Cold War Europe, NATO was related to crisis management and its role in broad-based comprehensive security cooperation was emphasised (Forsberg 2018). Secondly, the reference group for membership, consisting of eastern European countries, was considered distinct from Finland which positioned itself as a Nordic, or Western, country (Forsberg 2023, 43). Despite this, both Sweden and Finland declared their willingness to broadly cooperate with NATO through the Partnership for Peace Program (PFP) and via deployments to the Balkans, as these were considered essential for the European security structure.

EU membership had several positive implications for Finland – principally by allowing a route into the single market. Hence, for many, the main reason to join the EU was economic. Finnish businesses were able to trade more efficiently in the most dynamic region of Europe, and to benefit from common standards and regulations. Secondly, security-related reasons were also evident for many. Both explanations underline the relevance of material and security considerations, but from the constructivist viewpoint, the membership had wider relevance for Finnish identity and sense of belonging. It changed perceptions of Finland's position in Europe and in the world, giving Finland a seat at more important decision-making tables. Membership also confirmed and strengthened the Western identity and a sense of belonging to the same value community.

In the early 2000s, Forsberg and Vaahtoranta foresaw that changes in the Finnish and Swedish non-alignment policy would be likely to happen because of developments within the EU rather than because of changes in domestic politics or a threat posed by Russia (Forsberg and Vaahtoranta 2001, 88). Both countries became strong supporters of EU Common Foreign and Security Policy (CFSP). And, after the Kosovo crisis they developed the EU's crisis management capabilities. However, strong UN mandates for operations remained important for the Nordic states as they represented wider normative agreements in the international community.

From EU-framed military non-alignment to NATO

After Russia invaded Ukraine in 2022, the security situation changed dramatically. NATO membership was then seen as the best way to ensure Finnish national security (Arter 2023). Hence, an alliance was preferred instead of neutrality or military non-alignment. As demonstrated, domestic opinions on the matter had remained divided since the 1990s. Overall, only a quarter of the population had shown support for NATO membership (Nortio et. al. 2022; Weckman 2023). However, a change in public opinion after the Russian invasion was rapid. By May 2022, almost 80 per cent of the population supported membership. This is interesting, as the arguments during the four decades for and against membership did not materially change (Forsberg 2023). There were also citizens' initiatives to demand parliamentary action on the matter. Only the National Coalition Party and the Swedish People Party had declared NATO support before the invasion. Based on its report on changes in the security environment (Finnish Government 2022), the government proposed that Finland join NATO. Following the debate in the Parliament, in May 2022, its members voted (188–8) for Finland to apply for NATO membership.

Upon joining the EU, Finnish foreign policy acquired a new term: the 'NATO-option'. This option appeared in the government program of Paavo Lipponen in 1995 (a government of five parties, with both the Social Democrats and National Coalition). The program pronounced that Finland contributes best to the stable development of Northern Europe under the prevailing conditions by remaining outside military alliances and maintaining independent defence. The words 'under the prevailing conditions' were later understood and called as the Finnish NATO-option. Finland somehow had adjusted for NATO already in 1992, when Finland bought 64 F/A-18 Hornet fighter jets from the US. In 1994, Finland joined NATO's PfP Program. However, the foreign policy caution and the tradition of neutrality remained strong: In 1996, just after the pronounced NATO-option, the Defence Council stated that Finland would not apply for NATO membership.

After Finland's rapid entrance into NATO in April 2023, a long-existing Western-oriented anti-non-alignment opposition in Finland is more detectable. For example, the leading Finnish newspaper *Helsingin Sanomat* reported how Finland's NATO membership was realised as result of decades of work by its supporters (Teittinen 2023). According to Forsberg, the foreign policy elite (consisting of civil servants, soldiers, and security policy experts) became largely in favour of Finnish membership in the early 2000s (Forsberg 2023, 43). Such figures refer to the balance between East and West, disputes over military exercises and the arms trade, and how President Niinistö was perceived as too critical of the US and NATO. In the opinion of many, Finland could have given up neutrality in the 1990s, as Russian relations would probably have remained quite good. Prolonging the NATO application gave the wrong signal to Russia that Finland was its eternal ally (Teittinen 2023). The Finnish president meanwhile argued that what many experienced as slowness was instead diligence and justified caution, based on traditional Finnish prudent foreign policy (Niinistö 2023).

On the one hand, for many Finns, NATO's expansion in the North seemed an unnecessary provocation. At that time, the Finnish tradition of active neutrality still enjoyed wide support. There was also another reason – that NATO was not considered a major threat to Russia. In 1994, when Finland joined NATO's PfP Program, Russia was actually involved. On the other hand, the relationship with NATO was promoted in many places, and in many ways. Finland participated in crisis management operations in the Balkans and also joined the Afghanistan operation that followed the 9/11 terror attacks – which NATO led from 2003. The Finnish Defence forces sought networks, experiences and possibilities to have the best Western weapons, even though the Iraq War temporarily cooled relations between Finland and the US. Yet, the EU-based security policy served as a brake on NATO membership, even as various Eastern European nations, including Baltic States, joined NATO. In this light, the right reference group for Finland's comparison was Sweden, not ex-Warsaw Pact countries.

If one part of the political elite in Finland can be envisioned as quite critical of the US whilst holding a desire to 'understand' Russia – at least from the foreign and economic policy point of view – most high-ranking military officers saw Russia as a direct threat. In 2008, when Russia invaded Georgia, the pro-Western and pro-NATO Foreign Minister Alexander Stubb saw the war as a turning point, showing that Russia had both the desire and the ability to use armed force as a tool against its neighbours. Stubb stated that there were strong grounds for reconsidering Finland's membership in NATO, but he did not suggest haste either (Stubb 2008). Meanwhile, public opinion polls had kept the NATO-option alive in everyday discussions (Nortio et. al. 2022). In the end, Finland's NATO accession was approved amidst some critical voices arguing that various problematic aspects were not analysed and discussed in detail in the fast-track process. For example, the leading Finnish expert of international law Martti Koskenniemi has repeatedly criticized the legally vague 'strategic concepts' and the consensus mechanism in NATO which can significantly change some principles of NATO's policies and practical operations. Despite these critical arguments, the Finnish NATO-decision in 2022 reflected the essence of Finnish foreign policy. It was again (as so many times in earlier history) forged in the realist tradition, and by a wide consensus – and done so in contrast to Sweden's more identity-based foreign policy. At the same time, it is important to emphasize that in both Finland and Sweden, military aspects of neutrality took precedence over political ones. The traditional understanding of neutrality was broken because the military dimension now defined other policies.

Conclusions

Various external and domestic factors have shaped the position of Finland as a neutral state, and its model and interpretation of neutrality is unique. As we argued, Finnish foreign and security policy has been defined around three pillars: 1) relations with Russia, 2) Finland's own defence ability and sovereignty, 3) Finland's relationship with the West, including the neighbouring Nordics. This system is obviously defined by geography, built in a realist tradition and forged in historical terms with wide consensus. The Independent Finnish Republic adopted neutrality and looked first at Baltic defence politics during the 1920s and 1930s, and during the Cold War – despite the controlling Soviet gaze – relations with the West and the other Nordics was developed actively. After the Cold War, all the aforementioned pillars were maintained in some balance – and in accordance with the EU-based security policy. This was a new kind of post-neutrality. Finland became allied with the EU, but not militarily aligned. In 2022, when Russia invaded Ukraine, the Russian pillar had to be entirely rethought. Finland bid farewell to its long tradition of neutrality and became one of the most Eastern parts of the West and of NATO. Traditional neutrality was broken because the military dimension suddenly defined and overrode other aspects.

Finland's neutrality, founded during the early years of its independence, did not allow the country to escape from participating in World War Two. Finland's exceptional foreign and security policy was developed during the Cold War era as a necessity, and neutrality was a compromise. Internationally, Finland was closely aligned to common Nordic positions, even if domestic differences existed. Realist neutrality was the best and probably only option to balance between the West and the East, and a unique historical form of neutrality in Europe. Because of its specific characteristics, it cannot truly be seen as a model for others to follow. The uniqueness of Finnish neutrality is not only based on voluntary state preference but is largely driven by external and structural necessities. Finnish neutrality was always vulnerable as it was seen as suspect by both blocs, but for different reasons. Clearly, Finnish claims on neutrality have had both positive and negative connotations in history. On the one hand, it has hindered more active foreign policy and demanded adaptation and flexibility. On the other hand, the neutral position, especially together with the other Nordic states, has strengthened Finnish visibility and status at the multilateral level. Even if the meaning of the neutrality norm has evolved, it has left certain tracks and provided a continuity in the Finnish foreign policy approach.

This chapter has also revealed interesting differences between 'realist' Finland and its closest peer, 'idealist' or identity-based Sweden, a country with a more traditional margin of action than Finland. Even if both states adopted a neutrality policy, their attitudes towards it differed. During the Cold War, Finland was keen to follow Swedish leadership. But EU membership in 1995 changed this position. In its post-neutrality policy, Finland was eager to align more closely with the core EU policies than Sweden – for example by joining the European Monetary Union. Finnish non-alignment policy was developed in tandem with Sweden and strived for a more effective common EU CFSP and a closer NATO partnership. The Swedish-Finnish bilateral security cooperation was intensified already in the 2010s, but when Russia invaded Ukraine in 2022, Finland was more rapid in implementing its NATO option, taking a leading position most likely due to its different historical experiences, national identity, and domestic political culture.

References

Agius, Christine. 2011. "Transformed beyond recognition? The Politics of post-neutrality". *Cooperation and Conflict*. 46: 3, 370–395. https://doi.org/10.1177/0010836711416960.

Arter, David. 2023. "From Finlandisation and post-Finlandisation to the end of Finlandisation? Finland's road to a NATO application". *European Security*, 32: 2, 171–189, DOI: 10.1080/09662839.2022.2113062

Aunesluoma Juhana, and Rainio-Niemi Johanna. 2016. "Neutrality as Identity? Finland's Quest for Security in the Cold War". *Journal of Cold War Studies*. 18: 4, 51–78. https://doi.org/10.1162/JCWS_a_00680.

Brommesson, Douglas; Ekengren, Ann-Marie and Michalski, Anna. 2023. "From variation to convergence in turbulent times – foreign and security policy choices among the Nordics 2014–2023". *European Security*. https://doi.org/10.1080/09662839.2023.2221185

Browning Christopher S. 2008. *Constructivism, Narrative and Foreign Policy Analysis: A Case Study of Finland*. Peter Lang: Bern.

Finnish Government. 2022. "Government report on changes in the security environment".

Forsberg Tuomas, and Vaahtoranta Tapani (2001) "Inside the EU, outside NATO: Paradoxes of Finland's and Sweden's post-neutrality". *European Security.* 10: 1, 68–93. https://doi.org/10.1080/09662830108407483.

Forsberg, Tuomas. 2023. "Four rounds of the Finnish NATO debate". *Nordic Review of International Studies.* 1, 40–49.

Forsberg, Tuomas. 2018. "Finland and NATO: Strategic Choices and Identity Conceptions". In A. Cottey (ed.), *The European Neutrals and NATO. Non-alignment, Partnership, Membership?* London: Palgrave.

Forsberg, Tuomas. 2016. "Suomen NATO-politiikka konstruktivismin näkökulmasta. In Blombergs, Fred (ed.) *Suomen turvallisuuspoliittisen ratkaisun lähtökohtia.* National Defence University.

Hakovirta, Harto (1988) *East-West Conflict and European Neutrality*, Oxford: Clarendon Press.

Lödén Hans. 2012. "Reaching a vanishing point? Reflections on the future of neutrality norms in Sweden and Finland". *Cooperation and Conflict.* 47: 2, 271–284. https://doi.org/10.1177/0010836712445343.

Moisio, S. 2008. "Finlandisation versus westernisation: Political recognition and Finland's European Union membership debate". *National Identities.* 10: 1, 77–93.

Möttölä Kari. 2021. "From Aspiration to Consummation and Transition: Finnish Neutrality as Strategy in the Cold War". In Kramer, M., Makko, A. & Ruggenthaler, P. (eds.) *The Soviet Union and Cold War Neutrality and Nonalignment in Europe.* Lanham: Lexington Books. 210–232.

Niinistö, Sauli. 2023. "Presidentti vastaa kritiikkiin: "Voi olla, että olin liiankin tarkka". *Helsingin Sanomat.* 4 June.

Nortio, E., Jasinskaja-Lahti, I., Hämäläinen, M., & Pakkasvirta, J. 2022. "Fear of the Russian bear? Negotiating Finnish national identity online". *Nations and Nationalism.* 28:3, 861–876. https://doi.org/10.1111/nana.12832

Ojanen, Hanna and Raunio, Tapio. 2018. "The Varying Degrees and Meanings of Nordicness in Finnish Foreign Policy". *Global Affairs* 4: 4–5. 405–418.

Rainio-Niemi, Johanna. 2021. "Neutrality as Compromises. Finland's Cold War Neutrality", in Kramer M. (ed.) *The Soviet Union and Cold War Neutrality and Nonalignment in Europe*. (Lanham: Lexington books). 75–100.

Raunio Tapio and Tiilikainen Teija. 2003. *Finland in the European Union.* Frank Cass Publishers, Portland.

Stubb, Alexander. 2008: Speech by the Foreign Minister "The first post-080808 diagnose". 25 August.

Teittinen, Paavo. 2023. "Vaaran vuodet", report article in Helsingin Sanomat, https://www.hs.fi/politiikka/art-2000009558248.html

Tuomioja, Erkki. 2023. "Presidentti Niinistö on toiminut Suomen eduista huolta kantaen". Helsingin Sanomat. 6 June.

Uutela, M. 2020. "'The End of Finlandization". Finland's Foreign Policy in the Eyes of the Two German States 1985–1990'. *The International History Review.* 42: 2, 410–423.

Weckman, Albert. 2023. "Public opinion and NATO: How different security environments influence the support for NATO in Finland". *Nordic Review of International Studies.* 1, 4–24.

Wivel, Anders. 2017. "What Happened to the Nordic Model for International Peace and Security?". *Peace Review.* 29: 4, 489–496. https://doi.org/10.1080/10402659.2017.1381521

4

The Resilience of Irish Neutrality

KAREN DEVINE

Four out of five people in Ireland have consistently supported active neutrality as the cornerstone of Irish foreign, security and defence policies. Democracy, summarised as rule of the people, by the people, for the people – whereby citizens elect representatives to act on their behalf in accordance with their wishes – means that the Irish government should reflect these consistent, rational, public preferences for active neutrality in the conduct of foreign relations and activities. Yet, there is rarely an opportunity arising from international events that is not used by government party politicians in Ireland to claim that Irish neutrality needs to be looked at, debated, or abandoned.

This elite discourse first started in the 1960s, when the Irish government applied for membership of the EEC and was told by the European Commission and EEC member-state leaders to give up neutrality in favour of a European common defence and NATO membership. In response, the Irish government redefined its concept of neutrality to exclude the components of 'active', 'positive', neutrality and labelled this new concept 'military neutrality', comprising just one element – non-membership of a military alliance. In doing so, the Government entered into a 'two-level game' comprising two main strategic threads: a) lying to the people in Ireland about this redefinition of neutrality and consequent change in foreign policy orientations, and b) obscuring successive government ratifications of the policies, treaties and laws progressing European Union militarisation, because the people of Ireland rejected successive European Union treaties in referendums due to strong support for a concept of active, positive neutrality. This chapter describes the history, political context and reasons for the failure of the Irish government to fulfil the social contract on active, positive neutrality and the efforts of non-governmental players to expose, resist and reverse these developments.

Unlike the governments of Sweden and Finland, who have used the war in Ukraine as the foundation of their attempts to divest the last shreds of neutrality and officially join the North Atlantic Treaty Organization (NATO) in the absence of public support, the Irish government has not yet followed that same path. Why? To address this question, this chapter proceeds as follows: (a) an explanation of the two-level game framework based on a working hypothesis; (b) an analysis of each actor's preferences, drawing on a range of primary data; (c) reasons why each side has adopted their positions in the two-level game. The chapter concludes with a summary of the current state of play in the struggle over Ireland's active neutrality and European Union militarism.

Two-Level Game

Robert Putnam (1988) portrayed political leaders as positioned between two tables of (1) international negotiation and (2) domestic political forces. Putnam's two-level game concept provides a framework of understanding for the political agents involved in the struggle over Irish neutrality. In the framework, governments take decisions at the supranational level of the Council of Ministers of the EU (level I) to legislate for, fund and implement measures that eradicate all tenants of neutrality in the pursuit of a common defence and an EU army, whilst those same governments face political pressures at the domestic level (Level II) from the population and NGOs to stop the eradication of neutrality.

Figure 4.1 shows the two sides of the game: on one side, the European Union (EU), NATO, the military industrial complex, that together seek to eradicate Irish neutrality, militarise the EU and project power through military force alongside the university agents, think tanks and mass media promoting these same interests and goals (herein referred to in shorthand as the 'militarists'); and on the other side, the majority of people in Ireland, NGOs, the President of Ireland and a number of independent politicians that support active neutrality (the 'neutralists'). Each side has distinctly different concepts of neutrality and discourses that will be explained next.

Changes to Government Concepts of 'Military Neutrality'

The vast changes made by successive Irish governments under the radar of public opinion, in summary, include: (1) the reformulation and redefinition of neutrality, including its disassociation from peace policy, and policy reversals including (2) extension of EU political cooperation to military affairs. (3) Agreeing to the Western European Union (WEU)-EU merger. (4) WEU membership via the WEU-EU merger, and assumption of its mutual defence clause through the ratification of the Lisbon Treaty and in doing so (5) changing the meaning of the government's concept of 'military neutrality ' to mean 'membership of a military alliance' – the opposite meaning of the original 'non-membership of a military alliance' concept laid out in government white papers, etc., and a continued failure to inform the public of this fact. (6) Adopting offensive military operations dubbed oxymoronically as the 'sharp end of peacekeeping' through WEU Petersberg Tasks and NATO-led missions. (7) Joining the EU's Permanent Structured Cooperation in Defence (PESCO), the adoption of NATO military goals, and major changes in practice by (8) supporting wars in Iraq, Afghanistan and Ukraine. (9) Moving from a commitment to the UN itself to merely a commitment to the principles of its Charter, and all instigated under (10) a regime of meaningful silence on neutrality whilst substituting active, positive neutrality with a new foreign policy cornerstone of EU 'solidarity' (Devine 2008a; 2009; 2011). Similar changes to state discourses and foreign policy practices were carried out by successive Swedish and Finnish governments over the same time period in a coordinated process to eradicate neutrality (Devine 2011).

With respect to (4) and (5), Ireland, Sweden, Finland and Austria had formed a coalition and proposed the text of an alternative mutual defence clause in an attempt to avoid the inclusion of the WEU's mutual defence clause in amendments to the Treaty on European Union (Cowen 2003). The 'Big Three' (E3) of France, Germany and the UK rejected this proposal and inserted their own wording as Article 42 (7) TEU: 'If a Member State is the victim of armed aggression on its territory, the other Member States shall have towards it an obligation of aid and assistance by all the means in their power...'. This was the most significant moment in the two-level game, as thereafter, the Irish government rendered its original meaning of 'military neutrality' void by making Ireland part a new EU military alliance in 2009. The redefinition was covered up by the state and government in order to fit the square peg of the public's active neutrality preferences into the round hole of Irish Government decisions at the EU level, that include decisions to accede to the EU's collective defence structures and its ambitions for Permanent Structured Cooperation in Defence, and adoption of the goal of EU member-state soldiers undertaking 'the most demanding military missions ... acting in accordance with a single set of forces', i.e. an EU army.

Elite silences in Sweden (Christiansson 2010, 32) and Ireland (Devine 2011) on the mutual defence clause insertion into the TEU through the Lisbon Treaty amendments are meaningful. The European Commission's Lisbon Treaty booklet, distributed to the Irish public during the two referendums in Ireland on the Lisbon Treaty, was misleading in omitting any reference to Article 42.7's mutual defence clause – a remarkable silence given that the European Commission singled out the mutual defence clause as one of the most significant aspects of the Lisbon Treaty after it had been signed in December 2007. This is because it would 'allow the emergence of a true common European defence. It will introduce a mutual defence clause and a solidarity clause ...' (Barroso 2007). The EU's silence on the mutual defence clause is seen in the lack of awareness among the publics of EU member-states. The Eurobarometer 85.1 of 2016 shows only 12 per cent of European citizens claim to be aware of the mutual defence clause and to know what it is, driven by more males (17 per cent) than females (9 per cent).

A tension exists between the Irish elites' need to keep silent about the mutual defence clause and their desire to openly exploit it. For example, EU-funded spokesmen from the militarist side of the 'game' declared:

> Even if neutrality is defined by some political leaders in Ireland as simply meaning an aversion to military alliances, Ireland's commitment to the EU's Common Security and Defence Policy renders such a definition obsolete ... the EU is now a *military* [as well as a political and economic] *alliance*. A new government needs to explain why this is a good thing (Burke 2010, emphasis added).

Yet the continued line in public from those same university-based EU spokespersons, along with successive Irish governments, is that Ireland is not a member of a military alliance. These facts narrow the militarists' definition of 'military neutrality' to non-membership of a military alliance, meaning NATO. Table 4.1 compares the public elements of active neutrality to the government's current concept of 'military neutrality' and explains the stark contrasts in definitions of active neutrality and 'military neutrality' held by opposing sides.

The next section situates each actor within the two-level game: Firstly, the 'neutralists' who are the majority of people in Ireland, NGOs, the President of Ireland and a number of independent politicians that support active neutrality. Secondly, the 'militarists' – the European Union (EU), NATO, the military industrial complex, university agents, think tanks and mass media.

Active, Positive Neutrality and Majority Public Opinion

Table 4.2 summarises the results of nineteen opinion polls that asked about preferences on neutrality, military alliances and NATO from 1981 to 2023. It shows that roughly four in five people in Ireland consistently support active neutrality and just 13–15 per cent are willing to join NATO or reject neutrality. Both public attitudes in support of neutrality and the public's concept of active positive neutrality are stable over time and unlikely to change as they are based on the underlying values and identity of the mass public (Devine 2006; 2008b). The 1996 White Paper on Foreign Policy stated, 'the majority of the Irish people have always cherished Ireland's military neutrality and recognise the positive values that inspire it' (Ireland 1996: 118) and also recognised 'Ireland's foreign policy is about much more than self-interest. For many of us it is a statement of the kind of people we are' (Ireland 1996, 7). Yet, successive governments have regarded this consistent, values-driven public support for active neutrality as a barrier that needs to be overcome or bypassed.

Neutrality constitutes this general foreign policy profile or identity not just in Ireland, but for many other EU member state populations (Devine 2011, 356; Aunesluoma and Rainio-Niemi 2016, 60). Scientific modelling of Irish public opinion data shows values- and identity-based support for Irish neutrality; specifically, public attitudes to Irish neutrality, are structured along the dimensions of independence (*vis-à-vis* European integration) and identity (proud to be Irish) (Devine 2008b, 480). Eurobarometer polls have consistently shown that Ireland provides the largest proportion of people who a) regard membership of the EU as a 'good thing' and b) do not support a European defence – i.e. for the Irish people, being 'pro-European' means a rejection of EU militarism. For example, in the 2006 Eurobarometer survey (no. 66) Ireland comes top of the list of the member states in the proportion of people who hold a positive image of the EU, yet resides at the bottom of the same list as regards public support for a European common defence and security policy. Rather than being paradoxical, holding these top and bottom positions is compatible with the Irish public perception of the EEC/EU – as the militarist proponents intended – as solely a trade organisation. The former Taoiseach, Dr. Garret FitzGerald, together with the Fianna Fáil and Fine Gael political parties, deliberately painted the EEC in this way, taking care to smother debate on the EEC's political designs or military plans in their campaigns for people to vote 'yes' in the referendum on Ireland's membership in 1973 (Devine 2006, 157).

This fundamental difference in preferences between the public and the government in relation to the incompatible positions of retaining active, positive neutrality versus promoting and participating in EU militarism is the foundation of the aforementioned two-level game. Research into public voting behaviour in the referenda on the Maastricht and Amsterdam Treaties in the 1990s, and the Nice Treaty in June 2001 and October 2002, has shown that a significant number of Irish citizens have repeatedly voted to reject such Treaties furthering EU militarisation due to the erosion of the core tenets of active Irish neutrality (Devine 2009). The most recent iteration of the two-level game has been created through the Taoiseach Micheál Martin telling the European Parliament in Strasbourg (O'Leary 2022), 'we don't need a referendum to join Nato. That's a policy decision of government' – whereas legally, it is a decision for the people through a free and fair referendum. This potential public veto is the most important factor explaining the resilience of Irish neutrality to date. The reasons why people in neutral states do not want to be part of NATO are an important part of understanding this resilience.

Why do people in neutral states not wish to join NATO?

Looking from the perspective of neutrality supporters, there are several reasons to reject membership of NATO and by corollary, the aforementioned WEU-EU merged military alliance that is defined as the 'European arm' of NATO.

- The absence of control over the use of force and Ireland being automatically involved in war, e.g. 'a fear that joining a military alliance would mean automatic involvement in wars, without having a say or control over such decisions' (De Valera, Dáil Éireann, Vol.152: Col. 549– 51). This is a fear shared by other neutrals, including Sweden (von Sydow and Lindh veckobrev, in Eliasson 2004).
- NATO's resort to illegal use of force, without a UN mandate (e.g. Kosovo, Serbia, Iraq, Afghanistan, etc.) and NATO's commission of war crimes and failure to cooperate with investigations or cases brought in relation to war crimes and NATO states' refusal to be held accountable for NATO actions (ICTY 2000; ECHR 52207/99).
- Escalation of military activities despite public mass opposition and disapproval (Kreps 2010, 197).
- NATO's lead members (the 'P3' of the United States, France and the United Kingdom) undermining of the financial and operational bases for UN peacekeeping (Williams 2020, 482–3; Williams 2018). NATO countries have long disregarded UN command and control mechanisms, and have deployed very few uniformed peacekeepers to UN missions during the twenty-first century (Bellamy and Williams 2009).
- NATO's opposition to disarmament and demands for increased spending on arms procurement, in the context of its continued existence and expansion eastwards despite promises not to. For example, Ireland led the creation and ratification of the United Nations Treaty on the Prohibition of Nuclear Weapons in 2017, as part of a neutral's nuclear free zone parameters. NATO declared ratification of the Treaty as fundamentally incompatible with NATO membership (NATO 2023, Netherlands 2017), rejects the Treaty (North Atlantic Council 2017, NATO 2020) and pressured member-states not to sign it (Pimenta Lopes 2017). And, the European Union failed to adopt a position on the treaty (Devine 2020).

These are just some of the reasons why there is such staunch public opposition to NATO membership in Ireland, and these reasons are a resilience factor of Irish neutrality. The role of NGOs in supporting and reflecting the active neutrality preferences of public opinion is outlined next.

Active, Positive Neutrality and NGOs

The NGO sector's ability to challenge the hegemonic discourses of the state and its agents – including businesses, trade unions, media, think tanks and the majority of the political establishment – makes it an important actor within the two-level game system. 'I am here to be as objective as possible but I will say that the achievement of the "No" side was significant. It notched up a notable vote and saw a substantial increase after a substantial stable period', said Richard Sinnott in a presentation to the Oireachtas Sub-Committee on Ireland's Future in the European Union on 18 November 2008. He was describing the results of the activities of NGO protagonists behind the referendum campaign that resulted in a second public rejection of an EU treaty due to the public's desire to retain neutrality. Normatively, non-governmental organisations are a vital cog in the political machinery of direct democracy in Ireland and play a significant role in providing information to the public through pamphlets, public meetings and press conferences on areas of politics that are very tightly controlled by a tiny elite within governing political parties.

Table 4.3 lists the most active NGOs in the realm of foreign policy and neutrality. There are several coordinated and autonomous local chapters and affiliated groups within many of the organisations listed, as well as transnational movements at the higher level for cooperation, support and exchange; for example, International Committee of the Red Cross, Amnesty International, World Beyond War, and Human Rights Watch. Members are from across the political spectrum – most are internationalist in their views, well-travelled and highly educated. These organisations are issue-based and are not seeking to organise into a political party or obtain power within the political system (Lacey 2013, 129–135). Most activists – who come from all sectors of society, including students, private sector workers, the unemployed, trade unionists, retired civil servants, self-employed farmers, refugees, artists and musicians – carry out voluntary work for several NGOs. This is especially visible during significant political events such as referendum campaigns and in response to bespoke initiatives such as the government-organised 'Forum on International Security Policy' that was designed to produce a report demanding that Ireland join NATO and abolish the Triple Lock (a requirement for UN, parliamentary and government approval for Irish troops (12 or more) to engage in military operations) and all last vestiges of active neutrality.

Active, Positive Neutrality and the President of Ireland

In addition to NGOs, another non-governmental (but state) political actor, in the form of the President of Ireland, plays a role in the two-level game. The President is elected directly by the people and has two main roles: Firstly, the guardian of the constitution, and secondly the representative of the Irish state through mainly ceremonial duties. Although executive authority in Ireland is expressly vested in the government, the government is obliged to keep the President informed on matters of domestic and foreign policy. In that context, President Michael D Higgins (2011–) has given voice to concerns over various governmental attempts to eliminate facets of neutrality and commit Ireland to further EU militarism. For example, in 2018, a journalist noted:

> What might be interpreted as a public warning about neutrality to the Taoiseach, who is also the minister for defence, the President stated the government has a duty to explain why it signed up as a member of Pesco (Permanent Structured Co-operation), the EU's security and defence operation (McCarthy 2018).

Continuing this line of questioning in June 2023, Higgins reflected public support for active, positive neutrality in an interview (Whyte 2023) in which he questioned the selection of speakers at the government's four-day International Security Forum event – the composition of which was mostly made up of 'the admirals, the generals, the air force, the rest of it', as well as 'the formerly neutral countries who are now joining Nato' – and asked why there was no representation from still-neutral countries such as Austria and Malta. The President is correct in his observation of the biased selection of the invitees – indeed, aside from the military and other speakers from outside Ireland, every invited lecturer from a university in Ireland is either EU funded or a known government party affiliate. Just one speaker from the NGO called Peace and Neutrality Alliance (PANA) was permitted to contribute on the subject of neutrality. The President was critical, too, of the European Union for its increasing military posturing, citing French president Emmanuel Macron's comments that 'the future of Europe is as the most reliable pillar in Nato' (Whyte 2023).

Militarism and its agents

The university is now part of an unholy alliance that largely serves dominant state, military industrial complex and business policies, while decoupling vital aspects of academic knowledge production from democratic values and projects (Giroux 2007). The cohort of so-called Jean Monnet lecturers, who act as EU spokespersons in universities, are paid directly by the European

Union to be its 'intellectual ambassadors' (Weiler 2014) and are the main non-governmental agents dedicated to eradicating neutrality and overriding democratic processes and public policy preferences in Ireland. Wieler (2014) explains how such individuals carry 'ideological baggage' that contradicts their 'higher calling...as scholars ... committed to dispassionate critical enquiry without partisan political bias', and as a result, it is not possible to reconcile a Jean Monnet lecturer's 'instinct to defend [the EU] when [it] is criticized' with the pursuit of truth 'even if it is uncomfortable to the institutions, the funders of the Jean Monnet Programme'.

Figure 4.2 illustrates the public information of one example of a Jean Monnet university professor's biographical roles, funding, lobbying, and discourses on behalf of the government, the European Union and the military industrial complex. Six roles are shown in black circles whilst the red arrows reflect the interconnected funding and discourses. This United States-born individual started out affiliated with the Center for Strategic and International Studies (CSIS) Washington DC (1989–1991) (UCD 2015), a think tank that lists major funding from defense contractors such as Lockheed Martin (Smith 2020). Politically, as a self-declared party member since his youth (Tonra 1984), Ben Tonra occupied a position on the National Executive of the Fine Gael political party (Finlan 1988) – the party working for decades to eradicate neutrality and to join Ireland into NATO and the W/EU military alliance (Brennock 2003). Academically, he published a redefinition of active neutrality as 'Ireland's non-membership of existing military alliances' in order to make the claim that 'this policy of military neutrality has never been presented as precluding a defence element to European Union' (Tonra 1994). Tonra's claim is untrue because the EEC made it clear at every opportunity that neutrality precludes a European common defence. This can be seen from Jean Monnet himself, who placed 'advocates of a neutrality' in opposition to 'The Paris Agreements setting up the Western European Union...a traditional military alliance...[that] opened the door into NATO' (1978: 398), and in repeated European Commission official pronouncements on neutrality precluding participation in any purported EU common defence (European Commission 1967: 19, 1992a: 13; 1992b: 21, 23). These facts are referenced extensively in the academic literature (Maher, 1986: 140) and by the Government of Ireland (1996: 119–120; 143–144).

There followed a European Union award of a Jean Monnet Professorship (1999–2006) under the EU-funded Dublin European Institute (UCD) and then an *ad personam* Jean Monnet Chair in European Foreign, Security and Defence Policy in 2003 (UCD 2024). Further monies were accrued through Irish Government and EU-funded think-tanks, as a 'project leader' on security and defence for the 'Institute of [International and] European Affairs' (UCD Centre for War Studies 2010). In that capacity, Tonra told the Irish parliament, 'we must, as individuals, stop using the word "neutrality", which has nothing to do with our foreign policy' (Tonra 2008). In terms of work for the military-industrial complex, Tonra is a director of the Irish Defence and Security Association (IDSA), a registered arms industry lobbyist since 2021, and spoke at the 'National Security Summit Ireland' sponsored by arms corporation Lockheed Martin in 2022 (Cooke 2022). Tonra also established a consultancy called The Azure Forum that paid the IDSA 'to produce a report on the Irish defence industry' (Cooke 2022; Azure Forum 2024). The Azure Forum was appointed to the Commission on the Irish Defence Forces that issued a report demanding a 50 per cent increase in defence spending, with a view to trebling the budget thereafter (Commission on the Defence Forces 2022: 114). The IDSA met with the Minister for Defence to procure loans for military-industrial complex companies and obtain European Defence Agency (EDA) co-funding (The Ditch 2023). Thereafter, the Department of Defence facilitated the arrangement of a meeting between the EDA chief executive Jiří Šedivý and the IDSA in September 2023 (Doyle 2024). This illustrative example of one academic reflects links between the universities and the vested interests of the military-industrial complex, the European Union/NATO and governments and think tanks that together serve to undermine and deny public policy preferences for neutrality. Such action occurs not just in Ireland, but also in other former or currently neutral states such as Sweden, Finland, and Austria.

The blanket of Jean Monnet lecturer propaganda is carried through think tanks funded by the EU and its member-state governments, and saturates the mass corporate media. NATO prefers the use of third parties such as think tanks and academics to promote its agenda, rather than official statements (Babst 2009, 6). Take, for example, the proliferation of think tank reports on the Ukraine crisis since Russia's invasion in February 2022 – the EU currently lists over eight hundred such reports on its website (Council of the European Union, July 2023). That's a rate of 47 reports published per month. In Ireland, new EU-funded think tanks have sprung up, such as Azure Forum – described as 'a dedicated – first of its kind – peace, security and defence policy think tank based in Ireland' (Azure Forum 2023). This adds to long-standing groups such as the Institute of International and European Affairs (IIEA) and the European Movement Ireland. The crossover of personnel between think tanks, positions in universities, government/state bodies, and the European Union lays bare the power of militarism to control discourses through its funding of agents within the system, and makes it all the more remarkable how ordinary people in Ireland resist such anti-neutrality propaganda.

Moving to the media, the two trends pertinent for understanding the media's impact within the two-level game are (1) declining public consumption of media and (2) declining trust in what the media is saying. A 2022 survey found that 'overall news consumption has declined considerably in many countries while trust has fallen back almost everywhere' (Newman 2022). Forty-seven per cent of people in Poland, 46 per cent in USA and UK, and 56 per cent in Brazil actively avoid the news (Eddy and Fletcher 2022). Further, the media coverage of the Ukraine conflict has driven markedly increased news avoidance in places such as the UK, Brazil and Germany and a majority in surveyed states felt the media have not explained the wider implications of the Ukraine conflict or provided a different range of perspectives (Eddy and Fletcher 2022, 35–36). The link between lack of trust in the news media and increased news avoidance is clear, as 29 per cent of respondents who actively avoid the news do so because they think it cannot be trusted – while just a tiny minority think the media is free from undue political or government influence (Newmann 2022, 13–16).

In Ireland, the media employs three strategies of political gaslighting to destabilise and disorient public opinion on political issues and to shut down opposition to the war in Ukraine, promote militarism and eradicate neutrality: (1) propaganda, i.e. fear-mongering using unfounded threats; (2) code words, 'word play' and meaningful silences; (3) disinformation, e.g. false reports of opinion poll data and/or biased survey question wording. One example of the latter: a RedC poll asked respondents their view on a statement 'Ireland should join the North Atlantic Treaty Organization (NATO) to boost its security' – made in relation to the war in Ukraine – and a newspaper report on the poll made the claim that '48 per cent of people believe Ireland should join NATO to boost its security' (Brennan 2022). Firstly, the question did not ask the respondents their own personal opinion on the question, 'do you want Ireland to join NATO?'. Secondly, the statement's built-in implication that joining NATO boosts security is unfounded and arguably biased, given many claim the opposite is true – that NATO is an alliance that creates insecurity (Swomley 1949). The newspaper report also claimed the 'poll shows 46% in favour of Irish troops serving in [a] European army', specifically that respondents 'say they would vote yes in a referendum on the issue' (Brennan 2022). However, no respondent was asked about their vote in any referendum, let alone a 'yes' or 'no' on Irish troops serving in a European army – the question concerned an unknown person's opinion about a referendum on the question of troops serving in a European army.

Journalists reporting an Irish Times IPSOS poll claimed that 63 per cent of those surveyed were willing for Ireland to join NATO, shown in false pie chart graphics based on only those in favour of a change (Leahy 2022). The true figure of 15 per cent of all respondents was never provided either over social media or in print. All five opinion polls taken after the Ukraine war were manipulated or misreported in order to convey false levels of public support for NATO membership and EU militarism as part of a mass gaslighting and disinformation campaign designed to overcome public neutrality preferences.

Militarism and Government campaigns: The Consultative Forum on International Security Policy

In view of the perceived need by the government to justify the abandonment of neutrality against public wishes, it decided to host a so-called Consultative Forum on International Security Policy, with 'the invasion of Ukraine by Russia ... the context for the creation of the Consultative Forum' (mentioned seventeen times in the Consultative Forum Programme), in order 'to build a deeper public understanding of the evolving nature of threats facing the State ... and to examine the security options available' (Ireland 2023a; 2023b). The author of the report, written for the government, claimed, 'I believe that this was an admirably open and transparent process where unfettered debate was encouraged' (Richardson 2023). Conversely, a government party parliamentarian summarised it as 'a senior political force in government, side-stepping the participative democracy process we have (citizens assemblies) to hand pick speakers on a highly divisive subject and calling it a public debate' (Hourican 2023a); 'a deeply undemocratic forum' (Hourican 2023b); and 'an engine of disinformation' (Hourican 2023c). NGOs and neutrality supporters organised and attended their own forums, coinciding with the location and dates of the government forum, and made their presence felt.

Despite the report admitting that there is no public appetite for changing neutrality, the government proposed legislation on 22 November 2023 to dismantle the Triple Lock. The government introduced the Triple Lock as a 'safeguard of neutrality' to persuade the people of Ireland to reverse their decisions to reject both the Nice and Lisbon Treaties in referendums held in 2001 and 2008 due to the eradication of neutrality in the Treaties. The Government's Referendum Commission, headed by government appointee, Frank Clarke – who had actively campaigned for the Nice Treaty in 2001/2002 in support of the government campaign (de Breadun 2002) – informed the public that:

> The European Council has agreed that protocols will be added to a later EU Treaty to give full effect in EU law to these decisions .... an EU Treaty and any protocol to it becomes part of EU law and is enforceable. ... IRISH GOVERNMENT DECLARATION ... At the meeting of the European Council at which this decision was made, Ireland made a declaration in relation to military neutrality ... this declaration will be associated with the instrument of ratification if Ireland does ratify the Lisbon Treaty (Referendum Commission 2009, 23).

The wording was laid out in such a way as to have voters believe the Triple Lock would be in a legally-binding EU Treaty protocol if they vote yes in the second referendum on the Lisbon Treaty, and the government's campaign was fought on this basis. As stated in Dail Eireann, 'the triple lock became a central guarantee to secure the support of Irish voters for the ratification of the Lisbon treaty in 2009'. (Carthy 2024). The European Council (Presidency of the EU Council 2009a, 4 and 2) outlined the wording:

> The participation of contingents of the Irish Defence Forces in overseas operations, including those carried out under the European common security and defence policy requires (a) the authorisation of the operation by the Security Council or the General Assembly of the United Nations, (b) the agreement of the Irish Government, and (c) the approval of Dáil Éireann, in accordance with Irish law … (that was to be included in) … the [Lisbon Treaty] Protocol … to give full Treaty status to the clarifications set out in the Decision to meet the concerns of the Irish people.

The Triple Lock wording was never included in the Protocol (European Council, 2013), and as a result, has no legal protection. To hide this fact, it took the format of a 'National Declaration', with the EU declaring, 'In the event of Ireland's ratification of the Treaty of Lisbon, this [National Declaration by Ireland] will be associated with Ireland's instrument of ratification' (Presidency of the EU Council 2009b, 22–23). To dismantle the only legal barrier to sending Irish troops on high intensity NATO and EU military missions without a UN mandate, the government only needs to push amending legislation through the national parliament, in wilful disregard of public policy preferences, but, in doing so, the government will ensure that Nice and Lisbon Treaty ratifications are politically invalidated, provoking a democratic crisis of historical proportions.

Why are Irish Government leaders intent on securing membership of NATO?

This politically reckless and anti-democratic behaviour begs the question of what is driving government leaders to push legislation through the Irish parliament to destroy the remaining foundations of neutrality. One working hypothesis concerns the age-old problem of corruption. This issue has dogged the politics of neutrality for centuries in Ireland. In 1790 Wolfe Tone stated in his manifesto for Irish neutrality:

> Your innocence is yet, I trust, untainted by the rank leaven of corruption. Ye have no interests to bias your judgment but the interest of Ireland … direct your councils to … the establishment of the welfare, and glory and independence of Ireland for ever and ever (Tone in Devine 2013, 377).

In 1811, Irish nationalist leader Daniel O'Connell (1971, 53) conferred thanks on statesmen who 'had, with the purest patriotism, refused everything that power could give; they had rejected all the allurements of office, rather than sacrifice, or even postpone the assertion of principle'. Historically, Irish leaders have resisted the vested interests biasing judgment and betraying the interests of the Irish electorate. But, the current crop of government leaders are being promised well-paid posts in the European Union in return for popular betrayal. The current leader of Fianna Fail, Micheál Martin, is said to be 'the next Irish nominee for European Commissioner if he chooses. He has a longer shot at bigger jobs, including president of the European Council or EU High Representative for Foreign Affairs' (Howlin 2023). His own party's elected representatives have admitted they believe he is destined for an EU role in Brussels (O'Connell 2023). This view is widely held outside of the party also: 'There is a view held by some long-time Martin observers that he will resign this time next year and depart for Brussels, where he has been spoken of as a possible successor to Charles Michel as President of the European Council' (Leahy 2023). There is, evidently, contemporary precedence for ministers jettisoning neutrality for the EU's agenda and shortly thereafter occupying a position of EU Commissioner or EU ambassador (Devine 2011).

External elite influence in neutral states promoting NATO and EU militarism and warfare

Transparency International defines corruption as 'the abuse of entrusted power for private gains'. The relationships between government and arms industry corruption – and government incentives for launching invasions and wars, including proxy wars – are commonsensical for most people. According to Feinstein et al. (2011, 14), 'trade in weapons constitutes a mere fraction of total world trade, according to one estimate it accounts for a remarkable 40 per cent of corruption'. Arms corruption exists systematically between governments and arms dealers (Perlo-Freeman 2023). Three militarist protagonists – Angela Merkel (as Chancellor of Germany), Nicholas Sarkozy, (as President of France) and Jose Manuel Barroso (as President of the European Commission) – drove the Lisbon Treaty's finalisation of the WEU-EU merger, incorporating a renamed European Defence Agency for arms procurement, and enabling legislation for PESCO and a new Rapid Deployment Capacity EU standing army.

As France's president from 2007–2012, Sarkozy was implicated in a number of cases and in March 2021 was found guilty of corruption and influence-peddling to fund his 2016 presidential campaign. He was sentenced to three years in prison, two of them suspended (Willsher 2021). Another case involves claims that Muammar Gaddafi's Libyan government gave Sarkozy 50 million euros for his 2007 presidential campaign. Barroso's meetings with Ferrostaal to purchase two submarines, when he was Portuguese Prime Minister, were set up by a Portuguese intermediary who was convicted by a Munich court in 2014 (overturned on appeal in 2015) of collecting roughly €1.6 million as a consultancy fee (Perlo-Freeman 2017). This was one of dozens of suspicious brokerage and consulting payments made 'to decision-makers in the Portuguese government, ministries or navy' (Schmitt 2010). An ineffective Portuguese investigation was closed in 2014 with no convictions (World Peace Foundation 2022).

Foreign bribery payments were legal in Germany until the implementation of the OECD's Bribery Convention in February 1999. Bypassing German Political Contributions Law, the CDU *spendenaffare* was part of a broader pattern of secret political finance arrangements that had supported Chancellor Helmut Kohl's 16 years in office. Wolfgang Schäuble, CDU chairman, had been forced to admit to taking a 100,000 marks donation in his Bonn office from weapons lobbyist Karl-Heinz Schreiber on 22 September 1994. Six months after taking that bribe, Schäuble went to Dublin to announce that the four neutral countries in the European Union – Ireland, Austria, Finland and Sweden – would have to join NATO eventually, saying the EU would only have a real security policy when it became the European arm of NATO (Reuters 1995). Angela Merkel, who was party secretary throughout this time, was elected new chairperson of the CDU on 10 April 2000, one month after Wolfgang Thierse, the President of the Bundestag, fined the CDU a record sum of DM 41 million for faulty reports and party financing violations. As chancellor of Germany from 2005 to 2021, Merkel brought Schäuble back into her government cabinet as Finance Minister and together with Sarkozy and Barroso, they campaigned hard to militarise the EU.

All three EU leadership figures, Barroso, Merkel and Sarkozy, personally intervened in Ireland after the failed Lisbon Treaty referendum (Irish Examiner 2008a; 2008b; Hall 2008) using threats and intimidation to pressure the people of Ireland to vote yes in a rerun. Their collective efforts have enabled secondary legislation for the procurement of weapons using 'off-books funds' and designated middlemen (a member-state-appointed beneficiary 'procurement agent') (Council of the EU 2023: 20), whilst avoiding internal and international anti-corruption measures that will be used to support the proposed EU standing army. Public access to documentation related to the file is prohibited and requests to access the documents have been refused. These developments arguably show that the 'grave implications' of 'unwarranted influence, whether sought or unsought, by the military-industrial complex (a permanent armaments industry of vast proportions)' as voiced by US President Dwight D. Eisenhower (1961), are evident in this case-study on the resilience of Irish Neutrality.

Conclusion

Ireland's neutrality has been deeply rooted in Irish society and in decades of foreign and defence policy. The long-standing public attachment to active, positive neutrality, the consistency in the concept that accords with international law and the values of identity and independence underpin public support for neutrality. Despite this, top-down pressures exerted by elites within the Irish government, EU-linked institutions and beyond attempt to undermine the widely-held consensus on neutrality. A majority of the Irish population does not wish to join NATO for numerous reasons, including due to a lack of control over decisions and automatic involvement in wars; being wary of the conduct of NATO interventions; fears of illegal acts undertaken; a lack of political and legal recourse to arrest any notions of impunity; and the lack of responsiveness to public opinion against conflict escalation. However, as seen in this chapter, the government continues to work hard to stymie public support for active, positive neutrality, has not acted in accordance with democratic norms and has broken the social contract by failing to represent public preferences for neutrality. Three main drivers of these government failures are (1) differences in identification: the public in Ireland identify with their community and its needs, whilst government leaders identify with the European Union elite and its ambitions; (2) elite pursuit of material incentives of power and office at the European Union level in exchange for eradicating neutrality; (3) corruption, both legal and illegal. The two-level game framework enables a fuller and more realistic picture of the resilience of Irish neutrality. Ultimately, given the requirement of a referendum and the need to secure public approval of NATO membership, the government strategies for obtaining official, rather than *de facto*, informal membership have failed thus far. Finally, given the dynamics of oppression outlined in this chapter, the possibility that students, academics, and the general public can access critical evidence-based research on the topic of neutrality is highly constrained.

Figures and Tables

Figure 4.1: Opposing sides and their concepts of neutrality in the "two-level game".

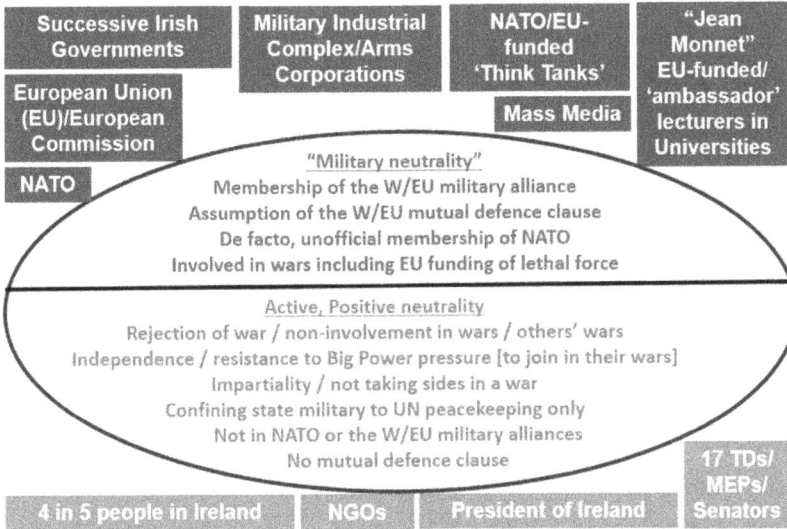

| Successive Irish Governments | Military Industrial Complex/Arms Corporations | NATO/EU-funded 'Think Tanks' | "Jean Monnet" EU-funded/ 'ambassador' lecturers in Universities |

European Union (EU)/European Commission

Mass Media

NATO

"Military neutrality"
Membership of the W/EU military alliance
Assumption of the W/EU mutual defence clause
De facto, unofficial membership of NATO
Involved in wars including EU funding of lethal force

Active, Positive neutrality
Rejection of war / non-involvement in wars / others' wars
Independence / resistance to Big Power pressure [to join in their wars]
Impartiality / not taking sides in a war
Confining state military to UN peacekeeping only
Not in NATO or the W/EU military alliances
No mutual defence clause

17 TDs/ MEPs/ Senators

4 in 5 people in Ireland   NGOs   President of Ireland

Figure 4.2: Case illustration of one academic's links to the national and EU Military Industrial Complex.

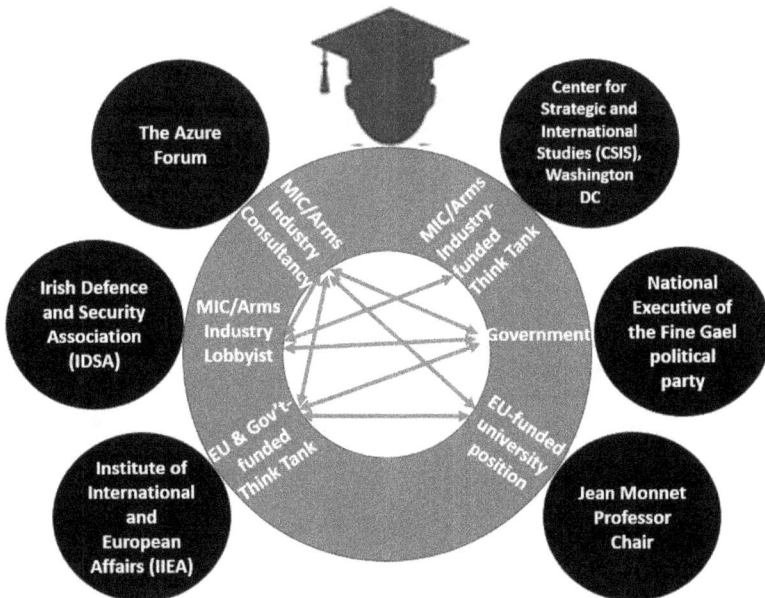

Table 4.1: Public Concept of Active Neutrality vs Government Concept of 'Military Neutrality'.

Public Concept 'Active Neutrality'	Government Concept 'Military Neutrality'
Non-Involvement in War	
Independence/resisting Big Power Pressure in decisions	
Impartiality/not taking sides	
Peace promotion/mediation	
Non-aggression/non-aggressive army	
Not join a European army'/not go to war if the EU does	
Peacekeeping only. No other military commitment	
Not part of [EU] defence / military alliance	
No NATO involvement/not in NATO	not [officially] in NATO

Table 4.2: Attitude to Neutrality and 'Military Neutrality' (%), 1981–2023.

Year	MRBI March 1981	MRBI April 1985	NUIM 1988/1989	MRBI Jan 1991	IMS Feb 1991	MRBI April 1991	LMR May 1992	MRBI June 1992	MRBI Sept 1996	MRBI June 2001	ISPAS 2001/2002	EOS Jan 2003	RedC Aug 2013	Amarach Feb 202 2	IPSOS Apr 2022	B&A Apr2 002	IPSOS Jun 2023
Alliance-against		64															
EU Military Alliance – against joining															68		
Neutrality-against dropping				64		65									71		
Neutrality-remain							59										
Neutrality-maintain	76								69	72							
Neutrality-retain			84					55			80	78					
Neutral status-hold on to													76				
Current model of 'military' neutrality – support															66		61
Gulf I - neutral				69	71												
Gulf II - military intervention unjustified												81					
Alliance-prepared to consider joining		25															
Neutrality-change								20									
Neutrality-reject											20		15	15			
NATO-join									13						15		14
EC Defence-join			25			28	19										18

Table 4.3: NGOs and political movement organisations supporting active Irish neutrality.

Peace and Neutrality Alliance (PANA)
Action from Ireland (AfrI)
Irish Anti-War Movement (IAWM)
Irish Neutrality League
Comhlamh, the Irish Association for Development Workers
People First/Meitheal
National Platform
Irish Campaign for Nuclear Disarmament (Irish CND)
Greenpeace
ShannonWatch
Catholic Worker Movement
StoP Swords Into Ploughshares
Connolly Youth Movement *Ógra Uí Chonghaile*
Veterans for Peace
Cork Neutrality League
Dochas
Pax Christi
Extinction Rebellion
People's Movement
Society of Friends (Quakers)

References

Aunesluoma, Juhana, and Johanna Rainio-Niemi. 2016. "Neutrality as Identity? Finland's Quest for Security in the Cold War". *Journal of Cold War Studies.* 18 no.4: 51–78.

Azure Forum. n.d. 2023. "Who We Are". https://www.azureforum.org/who-we-are/about-us/

Azure Forum. n.d. 2024. "Profile Ben Tonra". https://www.azureforum.org/ben-tonra/

Babst, Stephanie. 2009. "Public Diplomacy – the Art of Engaging and Influencing". *Speech by Dr. Stefanie Babst, NATO Deputy Assistant Secretary General for Public Diplomacy Strategy at the NATO.* PfP Symposium at NATO School in Oberammergau, Germany, January 22. http://www.atlantic-community.org/app/webroot/files/articlepdf/Babst_Public_Diplomacy.pdf

Barroso, José Manuel Durão. 2007. "The European Union after the Lisbon Treaty". President of the European Commission SPEECH/07/793 Delivered at the 4th Joint Parliamentary Meeting on the Future of Europe, Brussels, December 4. https://europa.eu/rapid/pressReleasesAction.do?reference=SPEECH/07/793&format=HTML&aged=0&language=EN&guiLanguage=en

Bellamy, Alex J. and Paul D. Williams. 2009. "The West and contemporary peace operations". *Journal of Peace Research.* 46 no.1: 39–57.

Brennan, Michael. 2022. "Poll shows 46% in favour of Irish troops serving in European army". *Sunday Business Post.* March 26. https://www.businesspost.ie/politics/poll-shows-46-in-favour-of-irish-troops-serving-in-european-army/

Brennock, Mark. 2003. "FG calls for State to abandon neutrality". *The Irish Times.* May 30.

Burke, Edward. 2011. "Strategic, Coherent and Constructive: Three Pillars for a New Irish Foreign Policy". In *Next Generation Ireland*, edited by Edward Burke and Ronan Lyons, 179–208. Blackrock: Blackhall Publishing.

Carthy, Matt. 2023. "Neutrality: Motion [Private Members]". *Dáil Éireann debate* Vol. 1046 No. 4, November 28. https://www.oireachtas.ie/en/debates/debate/dail/2023-11-28/17

Christiansson, Magnus. 2010. "Solidarity and Sovereignty – The Two-Dimensional Game of Swedish Security Policy". *Baltic Security and Defence Review.* 12, no.2: 26–49.

Commission on the Defence Forces. 2022. "Report of the Commission on the Defence Forces". April 8. https://www.gov.ie/en/publication/eb4c0-report-of-the-commission-on-defence-forces/

Cooke, J Vivian. 2022. "Ireland starts to get a military industrial complex: Too many speakers at the NSSI Conference pushed expensive weapons of war". *Village Magazine* August/September. https://villagemagazine.ie/wp-content/uploads/2022/08/Military.pdf

Council of the European Union. 2023. General Secretariat Letter to the Chair of the European Parliament Committee on Industry, Research and Energy, to the Chair of the European Parliament Committee on Foreign Affairs and to the Chair of the European Parliament Sub-Committee on Security and Defence, Proposal for a REGULATION OF THE EUROPEAN PARLIAMENT AND OF THE COUNCIL on establishing the European defence industry Reinforcement through common Procurement Act 2022/0219 COD, July 7. https://www.parlament.gv.at/dokument/XXVII/EU/148425/imfname_11269943.pdf

Council of the European Union. 2023. "Think Tank reports on the invasion of Ukraine". *Consilium Library Blog.* Accessed July 20. https://www.consilium.europa.eu/en/documents-publications/library/library-blog/posts/think-tank-reports-on-the-invasion-of-ukraine/

Cowen, Brian. 2003. "IGC 2003 – European Security and Defence Policy". Letter to Franco FRATTINI, President of the Council of the European Union. December 5. http://www.statewatch.org/news/2003/dec/cig62.pdf

de Breadun, Deaglan. 2002. "Bruton disowns colleague's EU tax plan: THE NICE DEBATE Referendum 2002". *The Irish Times.* September 18: 4.

Devine, Karen M. 2006. "Public opinion and Irish neutrality: a theoretical and empirical test of the 'rational public'". PhD dissertation. University of Dublin, Trinity College.

Devine, Karen. 2008a. "A Comparative Critique of Irish Neutrality in the 'Unneutral' discourse". *Irish Studies In International Affairs.* 19: 73–97.

Devine, Karen. 2008b. "Stretching the IR Theoretical Spectrum on Irish Neutrality: A Critical Social Constructivist Framework". *International Political Science Review* 29, no.4: 461–488.

Devine, Karen. 2009. "Irish Political Parties' Attitudes towards Neutrality and the Evolution of the EU's Foreign, Security and Defence Policies". *Irish Political Studies* (Special Issue). 24, no. 4: 467–490.

Devine, Karen. 2011. "Neutrality and the development of the European Union's common security and defence policy: Compatible or competing?". *Cooperation and Conflict*. 46, No. 3: 334–369.

Devine, Karen. 2013. "Values and Identities in Irish Peace Policy: Four Centuries of Norm Continuity and Change". *Swiss Political Science Review*. 19, no.3: 376–409.

Devine, Karen. 2020. "Nuclear Non-Proliferation and Disarmament in Irish Foreign Policy". *New Zealand International Review*. 45, no.4: 11–15. https://www.jstor.org/stable/48594703

Doyle, Paulie. 2024. "Martin's department set up meeting of pro-military spending group and EDA". *The Ditch*. February 24. https://www.ontheditch.com/meeting-between-pro-military/

European Court of Human Rights. 2001. *Grand Chamber Decision as to the admissibility of Application no. 52207/99*, 12 December. https://hudoc.echr.coe.int/app/conversion/docx/?library=ECHR&id=001-22099&filename=BANKOVI%C4%86%20AND%20OTHERS%20v.%20BELGIUM%20AND%20OTHERS.docx&logEvent=False

Eddy, Kirsten, and Richard Fletcher. 2022. "Perceptions of Media Coverage of the Ukraine War". *Reuters Institute*. June 5. https://reutersinstitute.politics.ox.ac.uk/digital-news-report/2022/perceptions-media-coverage-war-Ukraine

Eisenhower, Dwight D. 1961. "Farewell address by President Dwight D. Eisenhower" *Papers of Dwight D. Eisenhower as President, 1953–61*, Eisenhower Library. Box 38, Speech Series National Archives and Records Administration, January 17. https://www.c-span.org/video/?15026-1/president-dwight-eisenhower-farewell-address

Eliasson, L. Johan. 2004. "Traditions, Identity and Security: The Legacy of Neutrality in Finnish and Swedish Security Policies in Light of European Integration". *European Integration Online Papers.* 8 No.6. https://www. researchgate.net/publication/5014999_Traditions_Identity_and_Security_ The_Legacy_of_Neutrality_in_Finnish_and_Swedish_Security_Policies_in_ Light_of_European_Integration/link/00b49533cb1cabf99c000000/download

European Commission. 1967. "Opinion on the Applications for Membership received from the United Kingdom, Ireland, Denmark and Norway", COM (67) 750, Publications Office, Brussels, September 29. http://aei-dev.library.pitt. edu/1321/

European Commission. 1992a. "Europe and the challenge of enlargement". *Bulletin of the European Communities Supplement 3/92*, Publications Office, Brussels, June 24. https://op.europa.eu/s/ziTu

European Commission. 1992b. "The challenge of enlargement. Commission opinion on Finland's application for membership". *Bulletin of the European Communities, Supplement 6/92* Publications Office, Brussels November 4. http://aei.pitt.edu/1568/

European Council. 2013. *Official Journal of the European Union L60* March 3: 131–139. https://eur-lex.europa.eu/legal-content/EN/TXT/ PDF/?uri=OJ:L:2013:060:FULL&from=NL

European Court of Human Rights, *Grand Chamber Decision as to the admissibility of Application no. 52207/99*, 12 December 2001. https://hudoc. echr.coe.int/app/conversion/docx/?library=ECHR&id=001- 22099&filename=BANKOVI%C4%86%20AND%20OTHERS%20v.%20 BELGIUM%20AND%20OTHERS.docx&logEvent=False

Finlan, Michael. 1988. "Young FG hears genetic fingerprint call". *The Irish Times* February 6.

Giroux, Henry A. 2007. *University in Chains: Confronting the Military-Industrial-Academic Complex*. London: Routledge.

Hall, Ben. 2008. "Sarkozy all discretion on Dublin visit". *Financial Times*. July 21.

Hourican, Neasa. 2023a. (@neasa_neasa) "A senior political force in gov, side stepping the participative democracy process we have (citizens assemblies) to hand pick speakers on a highly divisive subject and calling it public debate". Twitter/X June 22. https://twitter.com/neasa_neasa/status/1673647163723911168

Hourican, Neasa. 2023b. (@neasa_neasa) "Deeply Undemocratic Forum". Twitter/X June 28. https://twitter.com/neasa_neasa/status/1674104843567235075

Hourican, Neasa. 2023c. (@neasa_neasa) "Engine of Disinformation". Twitter/X June 27. https://twitter.com/neasa_neasa/status/1673647163723911168

Howlin, Gerard. 2023. "Is Europe beckoning for Micheál Martin?: The Tánaiste's next role could be in Brussels – or in coalition with SF". *The Irish Times.* May 23, 14.

International Criminal Tribunal for the Former Yugoslavia (ICTY) Tribunal. 2000. *Final Report.* June 13. https://www.icty.org/en/press/final-report-prosecutor-committee-established-review-nato-bombing-campaign-against-federal

Ireland. 1996. *White Paper on Foreign Policy.* Dublin: Stationary Office.

Ireland, Department of Foreign Affairs. 2023a. *Terms of Reference: Consultative Forum on International Security Policy June 2023.* May 30. https://www.gov.ie/en/publication/4f4ee-terms-of-reference-consultative-forum-on-international-security-policy-june-2023/

Ireland, Department of Foreign Affairs. 2023b. *Consultative Forum on International Security Policy.* June 1. https://www.gov.ie/en/campaigns/e2a6b-consultative-forum-on-international-security-policy/

Irish Examiner (anon). 2008a. "EC President campaigns for Lisbon Treaty Yes Vote". *Irish Examiner*, April 4. https://www.irishexaminer.com/news/arid-30358016.html

Irish Examiner (anon). 2008b. "German Chancellor Urges Yes Vote on Lisbon Treaty". *Irish Examiner*, April 14. https://www.irishexaminer.com/news/arid-30357675.html

Kirk, Lisbeth. 2001. "Solana: Neutrality is a Concept of the Past". *EU Observer.* January 17. https://euobserver.com/news/1291

Kirk, Lisbeth, 2001. "No Solidarity with Neutral Countries". *EU Observer.* January 19. https://euobserver.com/news/1314

Kreps, Sarah. 2010. "Elite Consensus as a Determinant of Alliance Cohesion: Why Public Opinion Hardly Matters for NATO-led Operations in Afghanistan". *Foreign Policy Analysis.* 6, no.3: 191–215. https://doi.org/10.1111/j.1743-8594.2010.00108.x

Lacey, Peter. 2013. "The 'People's Movement: EU Critical Action & Irish Social Activism". PhD dissertation. National University of Ireland, Maynooth.

Leahy, Pat. (@PatLeahyIT) 2022. "The base for these graphs is all those in favour of a change. Though that's clear in the copy we should have made it clear in the graphs too. Sorry". Twitter/X, April 16. https://twitter.com/PatLeahyIT/status/1514938558880047106

McCarthy, Justine. 2018. "President Michael D. Higgins first shots over Ireland's commitment to neutrality". *The Times.* October 18. https://www.thetimes.co.uk/article/president-michael-d-higgins-fires-shots-over-ireland-s-commitment-to-neutrality-2kgvhx9j5

Maher, Denis. 1986. *The Tortuous Path, The course of Ireland's entry into the EEC (1948–73).* Dublin: Institute of Public Administration.

Monnet, Jean. 1978. *Memoirs.* New York: Doubleday & Company.

NATO. 2020. "North Atlantic Council Statement as the Treaty on the Prohibition of Nuclear Weapons Enters Into Force". *Press Release 131.* December 15. https://www.nato.int/cps/en/natohq/news_180087.htm

NATO. 2023. "Arms control, disarmament and non-proliferation in NATO". February 27. https://www.nato.int/cps/en/natohq/topics_48895.htm

Netherlands, the Kingdom of. 2017. "Explanation of vote of the Netherlands on text of Nuclear Ban Treaty". July 7. http://reachingcriticalwill.org/images/documents/Disarmament-fora/nuclear-weapon-ban/statements/7July_Netherlands.pdf

Newman, Nic. 2022. "Overview and key findings of the 2022 Digital News Report". *Reuters Institute*. June 15. https://reutersinstitute.politics.ox.ac.uk/digital-news-report/2022/dnr-executive-summary

North Atlantic Council. 2017. "North Atlantic Council Statement on the Treaty on the Prohibition of Nuclear Weapons." *Press Release 135*. September 20. https://www.nato.int/cps/en/natohq/news_146954.htm

O'Connell, Hugh. 2023. "Micheál Martin controls his own destiny – but Fianna Fáil TDs think he could be Brussels-bound". *Irish Independent*. June 25.

O' Leary, Naomi. 2022. "Ireland would not need a referendum to join NATO, says Taoiseach". *Irish Times*. June 8. https://www.irishtimes.com/world/europe/2022/06/08/ireland-would-not-need-referendum-to-join-nato-says-taoiseach/

Perlo-Freeman, Sam. 2017. "German Submarine Sales to Portugal". Tufts University WPF Compendium of Arms Trade Corruption. May 5. https://sites.tufts.edu/corruptarmsdeals/german-submarine-sales-to-portugal/

Perlo-Freeman, Sam. 2018. "Arms, corruption, and the state: Understanding the role of arms trade corruption in power politics". *The Economics of Peace and Security Journal*. 13, no. 2: 37–46. https://doi.org/10.15355/epsj.13.2.37

Pimenta Lopes, João. 2017. "European Parliament. Question for written answer E-006486-17 to the Council. Parliamentary Questions: EU position on the Treaty on the Prohibition of Nuclear Weapons". *European Parliament*. October 14. https://www.europarl.europa.eu/doceo/document/E-8-2017-006486_EN.html

Presidency of the European Union. 2009a. "Ireland and the Treaty of Lisbon". *Brussels European Council 18/19 June Presidency Conclusions*. July 10. 2–4.

Presidency of the European Union. 2009b. "National Declaration". *Brussels European Council 18/19 June 2009 Presidency Conclusions*. July 10. Annex 3: 22–23.

Putnam, Robert. 1988. "Diplomacy and domestic politics: the logic of two-level games". *International organization*. 42, no.3: 427–460.

Referendum Commission. 2009. *Lisbon Treaty Extended Guide.* https://www.electoralcommission.ie/app/uploads/2023/04/Referendum-Lisbon-treaty-2009-extended-guide.pdf

Reuters. 1995. "Neutrals must join NATO – Kohl aide". *The Irish Times.* March 10: 9.

Richardson, Louise. 2023 *Consultative Forum Chair's Report*. October 10. https://www.gov.ie/en/publication/36bd1-consultative-forum-chairs-report/

Sinnott, Richard. 2008. "Discussion with Professor Richard Sinnott". *Oireachtas Joint Committee on European Affairs (Sub-Committee on Ireland's Future in the European Union.* 192, no. 4 November 18. https://www.oireachtas.ie/en/debates/debate/joint_committee_on_european_affairs/2008-11-18/

Smith, Jessica. 2020. "CSIS Named No. 1 Think Tank in the United States". *Syracuse University News*. February 12. https://news.syr.edu/blog/2020/02/12/csis-named-number-one-think-tank-in-the-united-states/

The Ditch. 2023. "Department disputes defence lobbyist account of meeting with Simon Coveney". September 27. https://www.ontheditch.com/department-disputes-defence/

Tonra, Ben. 1984. "President Reagan's Visit". *Letters to the Editor. The Irish Times*. April 26.

Tonra Ben. 1994. "Ireland in European Political Cooperation: of substance over form". *Irish Political Studies.* 9: 99–118.

Tonra, Ben. 2008. "Ireland's Future Approach to EU Policy: Discussion". *Oireachtas Committee Debates: Sub-Committee on Ireland's Future in the European Union Debate*. November 11. http://debatesarchive.oireachtas.ie/Debates%20Authoring/DebatesWebPack.nsf/committeetakes/EUF2008111100003?opendocument&highlight=Ben%20Tonra11-11/

UCD Centre for War Studies. n.d. 2010. "War Studies Members Ben Tonra". https://www.ucd.ie/warstudies/members/bentonra/

UCD. n.d. 2015. "The state of the State: Prof Ben Tonra Jean Monnet Professor ad personam of European Foreign, Security and Defence Policy and Associate Professor of International Relations at the UCD School of Politics and International Relations". https://centenaries.ucd.ie/events/the-state-of-the-state/

UCD. n.d. 2024. "Professor Ben Tonra" and "Professor Ben Tonra Professional Activities." https://people.ucd.ie/ben.tonra/professional and https://people.ucd.ie/ben.tonra

Von Sydow, B. and Lindh, A. 2000. "Statement by Minister of Defense and Foreign Minister in response to comments by the commander in Chief". *Utrikesdepartementet Departements råd.* December 11. http://www.regeringen.se

Weiler, Joseph H.H. 2014. "President of the European University Institute, Florence Jean Monnet Conference 2014 keynote speech". *Jean Monnet Conference 2014: The Future of EU Studies.* 10–13. Luxembourg: Publications Office of the European Union. http://aprei.com.ua/wp-content/uploads/2016/11/Jean-Monnet-Conference-2014.pdf

Whyte, Barry. 2023. "Michael D Higgins exclusive: Ireland is 'playing with fire' in 'dangerous drift' towards Nato". *Sunday Business Post.* June 17. https://www.businesspost.ie/news/president-we-must-not-drift-into-nato-and-become-buried-in-other-peoples-agendas/

Williams, Paul D. 2018. "In US Failure to Pay Peacekeeping Bills, Larger UN Financing Questions Raised". *The Global Observatory.* October 23. https://theglobalobservatory.org/2018/10/in-us-failure-pay-peacekeeping-bills-larger-financing-questions-raised/

Williams, Paul D. 2020. "The Security Council's peacekeeping trilemma". *International Affairs.* 96, no.2: 479–499.

World Peace Foundation. 2022. "German Submarine Sales to Portugal". *Corruption Tracker.* September 12. https://corruption-tracker.org/case/german-submarine-sales-to-portugal

5

Bamboo in the Wind: Vietnam's Quest for Neutrality

NGUYEN KHAC GIANG

Since the collapse of the Soviet Union and the Eastern Bloc, Vietnam's foreign policy has gradually transformed from an ideologically-driven approach to a more interest-based one. In doing so, Hanoi has managed to overcome its isolation and deeply integrate into the international society. This integration has been achieved by normalizing relations with global and regional powers, particularly the United States and China, and actively participating in various multilateral platforms, such as the Association of Southeast Asian Nations (ASEAN) and the World Trade Organization (WTO), with a primary focus on economic integration. Through its neutrality and flexibility in dealing with great powers, Vietnam has greatly benefited from the post-Cold War world order. It has maintained strong military ties with Russia while enjoying access to the vast export markets of the West and reaping the benefits of trade with China. As a result, Vietnam has emerged as one of the top performers in terms of economic growth over the past four decades, all the while enjoying a relatively peaceful international environment. Hanoi has also become a leader within ASEAN.

Although not formally articulated in Vietnam's foreign policy doctrine, neutrality serves as a strategic cornerstone in Hanoi's approach to international relations. This principle has facilitated Vietnam's transition from a state of isolation to becoming an integrated member of the global community. Known as 'bamboo diplomacy' (*Ngoại giao cây tre*), Hanoi is lauded for its ability to ensure its own security without the need to align or 'bandwagon' with any major powers for a security umbrella. However, this approach is not without challenges. The increasing assertiveness of China poses one of Vietnam's most pressing security challenges, forcing the country to make difficult policy decisions regarding potentially closer alignment with the United States. Moreover, the inability of multilateral platforms like ASEAN to effectively resolve transnational disputes has limited Hanoi's options for achieving its foreign policy objectives without jeopardizing its neutral stance. The Russian invasion of Ukraine has strained Vietnam's longstanding military ties with Russia, its primary armament supplier, making it more challenging to balance relations with Beijing. Like other countries in the region, Vietnam is reluctant to choose between the United States and China. Nevertheless, as competition between these great powers intensifies, the option of delaying a decision may become increasingly untenable.

This chapter aims to comprehend Vietnam's foreign policy transition from Cold War bandwagoning to its current strategy of bamboo diplomacy. In doing so, it outlines the key characteristics of Vietnam's neutrality, the factors influencing its foreign policy decisions, and how Hanoi navigates its strategic autonomy within the uncertain geopolitical landscape of twenty-first century Asia.

From Communism to Pragmatism: The Pillar of Vietnam's Multi-directional Foreign Policy

Vietnam presents a fascinating case study which encapsulates the shifting dynamics of the global world order. This ranges from the post-Second World War independence movements to the intense superpower rivalry between the US and the Soviet Union during the Cold War, then on to the peace dividend of the post-Cold War era, and finally to the contemporary resurgence of great power competition between the US and China. Over the same period, Vietnam's foreign policy has undergone a significant transformation, beginning with its revolutionary foundations, transitioning through an ideologically-driven approach, and ultimately evolving into a framework deeply rooted in pragmatism.

Since the declaration of Vietnamese independence in 1945, extending through to its unification in 1975, Vietnam's foreign policy was fundamentally dominated by ideology. This period, deeply rooted in the Cold War, was heavily influenced by communism, and diplomacy served primarily as a weapon in their battles for liberation, first against the French in the First Indochina War (1945–1954), and subsequently during the Vietnam War (1954–1975). As a fledgling communist state, Vietnam's agency in its foreign policy was significantly curtailed, with the course largely charted by its larger allies – China and the Soviet Union. This reality was starkly evident in the 1954 Geneva Convention, which resulted in the partition of North and South Vietnam after France's defeat in Dien Bien Phu. This outcome satisfied the interests of major powers like the Soviet Union, the US, and China, but left Hanoi greatly disillusioned, setting the stage for another two decades of war.

The shift in Vietnam's foreign policy began post-1975, following the Fall of Saigon and the country's unification. Bolstered, and perhaps overconfident, by victory, Vietnam sought greater autonomy in international relations, as evidenced when it joined the Non-Aligned Movement (NAM) in 1976, signalling a desire for a larger role within the communist bloc. However, conflicts, notably with the invasion of Cambodia to overthrow the Khmer Rouge in 1978 and the subsequent Chinese invasion of Vietnam in 1979, disrupted these aspirations. The resulting international blockade and consistent northern threats compelled Vietnam to tighten its relationship with the Soviet Union. Upon signing an alliance in 1978, Vietnam effectively became a regional satellite of the Soviet Union, often dubbed the 'little Soviet Union'.

The end of the Cold War prompted another transformation in Vietnam's foreign policy. Left isolated following the Soviet Union's collapse, communist Vietnam had to rethink its strategy for survival. Initially, Hanoi sought to collaborate with Beijing in reinvigorating dwindling global communist movements. But when faced with a lukewarm response from China, which said it considered Hanoi as a comrade but not an ally, Vietnam came to the realization that to survive and prosper in the new world order, an ideological approach to foreign policy would not suffice (Tung 2021). This insight sparked a strategic reorientation in Hanoi's foreign policy, transitioning from revolutionary communism to pragmatism (Vu 2016).

This shift manifested with the normalization of relations with former adversaries – China and the United States – in 1991 and 1995, respectively. Vietnam began participating in various international organizations, from the World Trade Organization to regional platforms such as the Asia-Pacific Economic Cooperation (APEC), the Asia-Europe Meeting (ASEM), and ASEAN. In this diplomatic era, Vietnam re-established and maintained relations across a broad spectrum, from autocratic states such as North Korea to advanced capitalist countries it once considered adversaries. This pragmatic approach allowed Vietnam to benefit significantly from the post-Cold War 'peace dividend', boasting an economic growth rate surpassed only by China over the past four decades. Vietnam has emerged as a new Asian tiger, drawing substantial foreign direct investment from around the world.

Despite its communist roots, Vietnam's relations with fellow communist nations such as North Korea and Cuba have been minimized, further underscoring its turn towards pragmatic foreign policy. Aside from symbolic exchanges, these countries play no significant role in Vietnam's foreign policy calculations. For the world's remaining communist nations – Laos and China – Hanoi's relations are driven more by geopolitical and economic considerations than by ideology.

Vietnam has achieved success with its strategic adjustments in the post-Cold War era, effectively safeguarding its main national interests. However, the evolving geopolitical landscape in East Asia and globally, characterized by China's ascent and increasing maritime tensions, presents fresh challenges. Particularly, incidents such as China's 2014 deployment of an oil rig into Vietnam's Exclusive Economic Zone (EEZ), the introduction of China's self-proclaimed nine-dash line claiming 80 per cent of the South China Sea, and its aggressive land reclamation and militarization of regional waters have put Vietnam's neutrality policy under strain. While the Permanent Court of Arbitration (PCA) rejected China's claims in a 2016 ruling, it could not halt Beijing's ambitions. As security concerns gain prominence, the question of how Vietnam can maintain its 'neutral' stance in an increasingly polarized world comes to the fore.

Bamboo Diplomacy: Neutrality With Vietnamese Characteristics

The term 'neutrality' (*trung lập*) is not positively viewed within the context of Vietnamese foreign policy. Official documentation never labels Vietnam as a 'neutral state'. Instead, Vietnamese thinkers and writers – both within and outside the regime's framework – often use the term to depict countries with inadequate defensive capabilities that rely on astute diplomatic manoeuvring for survival (e.g. Cambodia, Finland, Switzerland, and Sweden). For instance, in its coverage of the Finnish elections in 2015, the Vietnam News Agency praised Finland as a 'small nation' for its wisdom in not 'aggressively rearming itself' and maintaining a delicate balance between NATO and Russia (Vietnam News Agency 2015). Moreover, when the Russian invasion of Ukraine occurred, several state-affiliated commentators criticized Kyiv for abandoning 'neutrality' and moving too close to the West (Dung 2022). In this context, neutrality signifies passivity in defence policy and vulnerability amidst great power competitions.

Conversely, 'neutrality' can also refer to states that implement a robust pragmatic foreign policy to maximize their interests, a descriptor often applied to Thailand and Singapore, particularly during the Cold War. In both interpretations, neutrality implies pragmatism and the absence of idealism.

Hanoi, identifying itself as a socialist state, believes that foreign policy must align with the state's political ideology. This was evident during the Cold War, as Vietnam adopted a revolutionary foreign policy, but has been challenging to implement following the collapse of the communist bloc and Vietnam's deep integration into global society. Consequently, there is a noticeable incongruity between Hanoi's intentions and its actions in post-Cold War foreign policy.

Despite Hanoi's commendation of communism, its relationships with its former allies are largely symbolic. While Russia is one of the only six countries that share a 'comprehensive strategic partnership' with Vietnam, their bilateral relationship – in terms of culture, trade, or investment – falls short compared to those with countries like the United States or Japan, two of Vietnam's former democratic enemies. Moscow remains crucial for Hanoi in two strategic areas, namely oil exploration in the South China Sea and weapon supply. However, both are under considerable challenges in the wake of the Russian invasion of Ukraine.

Besides exchanging ceremonial greetings on special occasions, Hanoi lacks substantial economic ties with the remaining communist states of Cuba and North Korea. Its relations with the other two communist nations, China and Laos, are driven by economic and geopolitical needs rather than ideological ties. In fact, since the end of the Cold War, Vietnam's foreign policy has increasingly prioritized national interest and pragmatism over ideology (Thayer 2018, 24). In an effort to reconcile the discrepancy between ideology and pragmatism, Vietnamese foreign policy thinkers have attempted to integrate traditional factors into the post-Cold War equation. This is apparent when examining how the Vietnam Communist Party (VCP) addresses foreign policy in its political reports, which represent the country's key grand strategy documents and guide all major policy decisions for the subsequent five years.

During the 7th Party Congress in 1991, just a few months before the collapse of the Soviet Union, the focus remained on Vietnam's relationships with key communist states and on its 'class solidarity' with communist movements around the world (Vietnamese Communist Party 2006, 75–76). However, since then communist objectives in foreign policy have been gradually supplanted by more nationalist goals. By the time of the 12th and 13th Congresses (in 2016 and 2021 respectively), the prevailing theme in Vietnamese foreign policy had shifted towards multilateralism, respect for international law, protection of national interest and identity, and deeper integration into regional and international communities. Cooperation with other communist movements and parties is mentioned only in passing, and with a stipulation that it should be carried out 'on the basis of national interest'.

In terms of military policy, Hanoi upholds a rigid 'Four No's' policy (originally the 'Three No's,' with the final point added in 2020). This policy asserts: 'no participation in military alliances, no alignment with one country against another, no hosting of foreign military bases on Vietnamese territory or using Vietnam as a fulcrum to counteract other countries, and no use or threat of force in international relations'. These various aspects make Vietnam's foreign policy quite similar to that of a 'neutral' state. However, since 'neutrality' is not a favoured concept, a new interpretation of Vietnam's foreign policy is necessary.

Vietnamese foreign policy thinkers have adeptly navigated this tricky balance, maintaining ideological integrity while promoting pragmatism under the banner of 'Ho Chi Minh thought' (Vu Khoan 2015). Party theorists have defined Ho Chi Minh's thought in foreign policy as an emphasis on multilateralism, strategic autonomy, and policy flexibility (Tuan 2015), traits closely aligned with 'neutrality'. After the 12th Party Congress in 2016, the conceptualization of Vietnam's foreign policy was developed even further, focusing on two main concepts: strategic autonomy (Tự chủ chiến lược) and 'bamboo diplomacy' (ngoại *giao cây tre*). The latter term was especially publicized after VCP General Secretary Nguyen Phu Trong used the term publicly in late 2021.

Vietnam's interpretation of 'bamboo diplomacy', akin to that of Thailand's, symbolizes its inherent flexibility and resilience. Despite the strong winds of geopolitical tension, Vietnam has managed to bend without breaking, sustaining robust military relations with Russia, opening its doors to the massive export markets of the Western world, and maintaining vital trade relationships with China. This unique approach has created a conducive environment that allowed Vietnam to emerge as one of the world's top economic performers over the past four decades.

Vietnam's bamboo diplomacy puts a premium on multilateralism, with a special focus on regional integration. As a country that was ensnared in bloody proxy wars throughout the twentieth century, Hanoi has entirely renounced the 'bandwagon' strategy. Instead, it relies on a robust network of friendships and partnerships based on mutual interests (Giang 2022). A notable Vietnamese policy thinker once remarked that among the 60 countries possessing 'significant national power', Vietnam needs to establish sound cooperation frameworks with at least half of them in order to safeguard its interests (Tran Viet Thai 2015). As of 2024, Vietnam has established various degrees of partnerships with a multitude of countries. In hierarchical order, these include three 'special partnerships', seven 'comprehensive strategic partnerships' (CSPs) – with Russia, China, India, and South Korea, the US, Australia, and Japan – eleven 'strategic partnerships', and twelve 'comprehensive partnerships'. Each category defines the extent of cooperation Vietnam is willing to engage in with its partners. The 'special' category only refers to three countries which Hanoi had special relations during the years of the wars of independence (Laos, Cambodia, and Cuba). A comprehensive partnership typically emphasizes collaboration in non-security areas like economic cooperation, trade, and cultural exchanges. Conversely, CSPs theoretically permit a fully comprehensive approach, meaning governments at all levels can collaborate with their CSPs on a wide range of topics without any restrictions, even in sensitive areas such as intelligence-sharing or defence cooperation. In particular, the double-upgrade in bilateral ties with the US, from comprehensive partnership to CSP level in September 2023, marked a significant milestone in Vietnam's 'bamboo diplomacy'.

Despite some dismissals of the Association of Southeast Asian Nations (ASEAN) as inconsequential amidst the re-emergence of major power rivalry, this regional consortium retains paramount importance for Vietnam. Vietnam utilizes the ASEAN platform to voice its positions, engage with countries that share similar views, and rally international support in its efforts to counter China's increasing assertiveness in the South China Sea. Enhanced ASEAN-led forums, such as the East Asia Summit (EAS) and the ASEAN Regional Forum (ARF), provide venues for discussions on sensitive topics that may be too delicate for bilateral conversations.

Hanoi's approach to multilateralism invariably involves trade. With a trade-to-GDP ratio nearing 200 per cent, Vietnam has become one of the world's most trade-dependent economies. The country is a party to 15 free trade agreements (FTAs), including the rigorous EU-Vietnam FTA (EVFTA), signed in 2019, and the expansive Comprehensive and Progressive Agreement for Trans-Pacific Partnership (CPTPP), established in 2018.

Second, as a smaller state, Vietnam remains committed to international law, especially the United Nations Charter and relevant conventions. In the wake of the Russian invasion of Ukraine, although Hanoi didn't explicitly name Moscow, it implicitly criticized Russia by urging all parties to 'respect sovereignty and independence' as stipulated in the UN Charter. In its struggle with China's increasing assertiveness regarding the South China Sea, Vietnam consistently advocates resolving disputes based on international law, particularly the United Nations Convention on the Law of the Sea (UNCLOS) 1982.

Third, Vietnam places significant emphasis on economic and trade relations as the primary focal point of its diplomacy. Hanoi views economic development as a less contentious issue, making it more amenable to compromise compared to other aspects of foreign policy. Consequently, Vietnam has actively pursued the signing of numerous free trade agreements (FTAs), having accumulated 19 FTAs by 2023, with three more currently under negotiation. Vietnam is regarded as one of the most trade-friendly nations globally, with a trade-to-GDP ratio of approximately 200 per cent, placing it second in Asia only to Singapore. This economic pragmatism allows Vietnam to swiftly overcome ideological differences and past grievances, leading to the United States and the European Union emerging as its primary and secondary export markets, respectively.

Fourth, Vietnam's bamboo diplomacy implies proactive engagement rather than passivity, with a specific focus on niche diplomacy where it has the capacity to exert influence, such as climate change, peacebuilding, and transnational water management (Do 2022). This proactive approach is crucial because, given its limited influence and resources, Hanoi must utilize them wisely. In doing so, Vietnam assumes the role of a middle power with a strong sense of agency. This distinguishes Vietnam's 'bamboo diplomacy' from the approaches of other 'neutral' states. During a Centre for Strategic Studies (CSIS) speech in May 2022, Vietnamese Prime Minister Pham Minh Chinh, when asked about which side Vietnam was on in the Ukrainian war, stated that Vietnam does not pick sides but stands for 'justice'. This statement reaffirms Hanoi's emphasis on adhering to international law, particularly the UN Charter, even though it did not explicitly criticize Russia by name.

Vietnam's bamboo diplomacy exhibits certain similarities to Thailand's approach, but there are notable differences between the two. First, while Thailand considers itself a 'small power that can never...make a significant impact on the system' (Busbarat 2016, 236), resulting in a tendency to be less proactive and more reactive to geopolitical changes, Vietnam has been keen on taking diplomatic initiatives, particularly in the last decade (2014–2024). It organized the historic Donald Trump-Kim Jong Un summit in Hanoi in 2019 and has been a driving force for a more proactive stance within ASEAN on regional issues. Vietnam has also actively participated in UN activities, including peacekeeping operations, and served as a non-permanent member of the UN Security Council twice, first in 2008–2009 and then in 2020–2021. In contrast, Thailand's last tenure on the Security Council was during the Cold War in 1985–1986. Second, due to ideological restrictions, Vietnam's foreign policy has less room for manoeuvre compared to Thailand. For instance, while Thailand was able to shift from being a neutral state after the Second World War to adopting an anti-communist stance during the Vietnam War, Hanoi did not have the same flexibility to deviate significantly from its ideological core as a socialist country. This explains why Bangkok can forge an alliance with the United States while maintaining close economic ties with China, or vice versa, while such options are less feasible for Hanoi. Third, Vietnam's geographical position as a neighbour of China, both on land and at sea, presents challenges to its pursuit of 'strategic autonomy' if it implies explicitly moving away from Beijing. This will be further discussed in the upcoming section.

Bamboo and the Dragon: Vietnam's China Dilemma

Vietnam's bamboo diplomacy had experienced significant success from the late 1990s to the late 2010s, benefiting from the post-Cold War peace dividend and a global focus on economic cooperation. During this period, Vietnam's trade-oriented economy thrived, with trade volume increasing from US$9.6 billion in 1991 to US$77.4 billion in 2007, the year it joined the World Trade Organization (WTO). Embracing multilateralism, Vietnam aimed to position itself as a regional middle power.

However, the dynamics have shifted with China's growing assertiveness and its pursuit of a 'peaceful rise' narrative to reclaim its status as a global superpower. As part of this vision, China has sought to consolidate its control over the South China Sea and exert influence over the Southeast Asia region. This shift has compelled Vietnam to confront China's expanding influence, which not only extends to Vietnam's own territory and waters but also impacts its traditional allies of Laos and Cambodia, which are crucial to Vietnam's security considerations. Consequently, Vietnam can no longer afford to overlook China's overarching influence and must navigate the complexities of this evolving geopolitical landscape.

To counter China's influence, Hanoi has adopted a comprehensive set of policies as part of its grand strategy. These policies encompass various approaches, including economic pragmatism, direct engagement, hard balancing, and soft balancing (Le Hong 2013). First, economic pragmatism is evident in Vietnam's approach. Despite concerns over China's influence, Vietnam continues to develop a deeply intertwined economic relationship with its neighbour. China remains Vietnam's largest trading partner, and its economic link with China remains vital in Hanoi's development strategy. Second, direct engagement is pursued when necessary. Vietnam maintains both party-to-party and state-to-state channels of communication with China. These engagements serve to manage bilateral issues and de-escalate tensions, particularly in times of crisis such as the oil rig incident in 2014. Third, hard balancing is a key aspect of Vietnam's strategy. Hanoi recognizes the importance of modernising its military capabilities, particularly in the context of maritime defence. Vietnam has invested in improving its naval capabilities and maritime infrastructure to enhance its ability to protect its territorial integrity and interests in the South China Sea. Lastly, soft balancing is employed as Vietnam seeks to constrain China's freedom of action. Hanoi actively reaches out to external partners, both within the region and beyond, to foster relationships and cooperation. By building a strong web of friends and partners, Vietnam aims to create a network of support that can provide a counterbalance to China's influence.

The final aspect of Vietnam's strategy to counter China's influence includes seeking a closer alignment with the United States, cultivating relationships with other regional powers, and embedding itself in the liberal world order. Despite a history of conflict, the relationship between Vietnam and the US has significantly improved. The US has become Vietnam's largest export market, a preferred destination for Vietnamese students studying abroad, and holds a positive image in the eyes of the Vietnamese public. In public polling by Pew Research Centre, Vietnam has always topped the list of the countries which view the US most positively. This might be attributed to the public perception of Washington as being aligned with Vietnam in its maritime disputes in the South China Sea with China, the perception of the US as a formidable economic power, and the perception of American society as desirable. The comprehensive partnership between the two countries extends beyond mere symbolism, with increasing levels of diplomatic, military, and intelligence cooperation. Vietnam sees the US as a significant counterbalance to China's influence in the South China Sea and leverages its relationship with Washington to manage its relations with Beijing.

In addition to the US, Vietnam seeks closer relationships with other regional powers. This includes potential great powers such as India, economic great powers like Japan, and active middle powers such as South Korea and Australia. By cultivating partnerships with these countries, Vietnam aims to establish a network of friends and allies that can provide support and assistance in times of need, particularly in dealing with challenges posed by China. Vietnam also aligns itself with the liberal world order by actively participating in multilateral institutions and emphasising the importance of international law and order. Vietnam's approach to addressing disputes, particularly those related to China's excessive claims in the South China Sea, is rooted in the principles of UNCLOS. By adhering to international norms and using legal frameworks, Vietnam seeks to uphold the rule of law and maintain its position within the existing liberal world order.

Vietnam continues to face a dilemma in its relationship with China. Despite its inclination towards the US, China still exerts a significant influence on Vietnam's foreign policy. Beijing has various means to pressure Hanoi into compliance, such as deploying maritime forces alongside research vessels or oil rigs deep into Vietnamese Exclusive Economic Zone (EEZ), using the China Coast Guard to harass Vietnamese fishing vessels, or imposing informal economic coercive measures by suddenly closing border gates. China accounts for more than half of Vietnam's agricultural exports, which is significant for a country where half the population live in the countryside. Furthermore, despite territorial disputes, the communist parties of Vietnam and China maintain an ideological bond rooted in their shared history. China was a primary financial supporter of Hanoi during its wars of independence against France and the United States, until a shift in policy after the China-US rapprochement in 1972 altered their relationship. In the post-Soviet era, China remains the sole communist nation that Vietnam can draw lessons from. Beijing capitalises on this, exploiting the Vietnamese party's apprehension of regime change to create divisions in the emerging Vietnam-US partnership and stoke fears of potential 'colour revolutions' (Giang 2022). Lingering scars from historical invasions, including the most recent conflict in 1979, contribute to a perpetual sense of security concern from the northern border. This concern likely explains why Vietnam and the United States have not yet upgraded their relationship to the level of a 'strategic partnership' despite discussions on the matter since 2018, as Hanoi is cautious about becoming an unintended casualty in escalating US-China tensions.

Concluding Remarks

Nguyen Co Thach, a former Vietnamese Minister of Foreign Affairs and a key architect of Vietnam's post-Doi Moi foreign policy, astutely remarked that countries like Vietnam are often perceived as mere pawns in international politics. However, he emphasized that even a pawn can survive and thrive, if it knows when to make strategic moves. Vietnam's current approach of active neutrality, or bamboo diplomacy, seems to follow this advice. Yet, as tensions between China and the United States continue to escalate, Vietnam's ability to maintain neutrality is becoming increasingly challenging.

China's assertive actions in the South China Sea, including the construction of artificial islands and constant harassment of Southeast Asian claimants, match its aggressive maritime claims. Vietnam, being at the forefront of these disputes, faces the most significant consequences. This is further complicated by the Russian invasion of Ukraine. Although Vietnam's economic and trade relationship with Russia may be minimal, Moscow plays a crucial role in Vietnam's hedging strategy against China. As Vietnam's largest arms supplier, Russia provides vital support to Vietnam's defence capabilities. Additionally, Russia is the biggest foreign investor in Vietnam's oil and gas exploration activities in the South China Sea, an area that has faced mounting pressure from China. While Russia continues to be Vietnam's largest arms supplier, payment difficulties and the risk of sanctions have made importing weapons from Russia increasingly challenging. Moreover, Russia's performance in Ukraine raises doubts on the effectiveness of its weaponry. Meanwhile, the alignment between Russia and China resulting from the Ukrainian invasion carries significant geopolitical implications for Vietnam. Moscow may be inclined to offer concessions on its cooperation with Vietnam in the South China Sea, which holds less strategic value given its current position, in exchange for China's support. Hanoi remembers well being abandoned by its former ally, the Soviet Union, in the Johnson South Reef Skirmish in 1988 – at a time when Moscow wanted to normalise its relationship with Beijing.

Recognizing the limitations in its bilateral relationship with the United States, Vietnam has turned to regional multilateral frameworks to pursue its foreign policy goals. ASEAN, despite its imperfections, offers crucial avenues for Vietnam to advance its objectives. Within ASEAN, Vietnam can voice its concerns, forge alliances with like-minded partners, and garner international support in countering China's increasing aggression in the South China Sea. Expanded forums such as the East Asia Summit (EAS), the ASEAN Regional

Forum (ARF), and the ASEAN Defence Ministers' Meeting Plus (ADMM+) provide valuable platforms for discussing sensitive issues that might be difficult to address bilaterally. Similarly, other platforms like APEC and ASEM also offer opportunities for engagement and cooperation.

However, traditional regional institutions like ASEAN also face big challenges. First, while its 'centrality' and non-interference principle might work well in a peaceful environment, that is no longer the case in an increasingly tense great power rivalry in the region. ASEAN fails to address pressing regional issues, from the South China Sea tensions to Mekong River-related issues. ASEAN's consensus decision-making process often hampers countries with shared interests from effectively working together, while providing a convenient platform for Beijing to sow discord, as demonstrated in its interactions with Cambodia in 2012 and Laos in 2016. These countries, without direct interests in the South China Sea, were willing to downplay the issue during their ASEAN chairmanship to secure China's favour, be it more concessional loans or infrastructural investments. Second, the rise of 'minilateralism' of exclusively security-centric groups like the Quadrilateral Security Dialogue (Quad, consisting of Australia, India, Japan, and the United States) and AUKUS also presents an additional challenge (Ha 2022). While Vietnam tacitly endorses these new security initiatives, which aim at containing China more effectively, Hanoi has legitimate concerns about the potential diminishment of ASEAN's central role. It does not want its security decided in either Washington or Canberra, similar to what happened during the Cold War.

Such developments have led policymakers in Hanoi to further prioritise expanding partnerships with other powers in the region. Among these, Japan and South Korea are Vietnam's most important economic partners. In the past decade, both countries have expanded ties with Hanoi into security cooperation, perhaps with an eye on China's growing regional ambitions. South Korea has joined Japan in this regard. Additionally, India and Australia have also deepened their defence cooperation with Vietnam. South Korea, which replaced Russia as the biggest arms supplier for Southeast Asia since 2022, is interested in Vietnam's arms imports market, which is trying to diversify from Russia. India, on the other hand, offers an attractive alternative for Hanoi, given that India has developed its defence industry based on Russian systems. These relations will also provide an effective backchannel for Hanoi to indirectly cooperate with the US on areas such as intelligence sharing or maritime security without overtly displeasing Beijing. The strong web of partnerships with other regional powers provides Vietnam with a broader platform for economic and political cooperation, opportunities to access advanced technology and capital for development, and a means to buffer itself against the potential pitfalls of an increasingly bipolar regional power structure, where its interests might be eclipsed by those of superpowers like the United States and China.

It is important to also note that Vietnam faces a multitude of challenges beyond geopolitical concerns. Chief among them is its vulnerability to climate change, with rising sea levels and extreme weather events posing significant threats to its populous coastal areas and its crucial agricultural sector. Moreover, Vietnam contends with a pressing infrastructural deficit that impacts its economic growth and quality of life, as the country struggles to keep pace with the demands of its rapidly growing economy and urbanizing population. Compounding these issues, Vietnam is also wrestling with deforestation, biodiversity loss, and water and air pollution, resulting from unbridled industrialisation and urban expansion. Many of these issues, such as the damming of the Mekong River, are transnational and require Vietnam to actively engage with multiple stakeholders. Internally, the Vietnamese Communist Party remains paranoid about the risk of mass uprisings that could challenge its long-standing rule. The country's increasingly well-educated, open-minded, and prosperous middle class may demand greater political rights and reforms. This adds another layer of complexity to Hanoi's strategic calculations as it navigates these issues alongside the external challenges mentioned in this chapter.

References

Busbarat, P. 2016. "Bamboo Swirling in the Wind": Thailand's Foreign Policy Imbalance between China and the United States. *Contemporary Southeast Asia, 38*(2), 233–257. Retrieved from http://www.jstor.org/stable/24916631

Do, T. T. 2022. Vietnam's Emergence as a Middle Power in Asia: Unfolding the Power–Knowledge Nexus. *Journal of Current Southeast Asian Affairs, 41*(2), 279–302. doi:10.1177/18681034221081146

Dung, P. T. T. 2022. Some explanations for the current Russia-Ukraine conflicts and strategic calculations of each side [Một số lý giải về cuộc xung đột Nga - Ukraine hiện nay và tính toán chiến lược của các bên]. *Tuyen giao [Propaganda]*. https://tuyengiao.vn/the-gioi/mot-so-ly-giai-ve-cuoc-xung-dot-nga-ukraine-hien-nay-va-tinh-toan-chien-luoc-cua-cac-ben-138175

Giang, N. K. 2022. US-Vietnam partnership goes beyond strategic competition with China. *United States Institute of Peace.*

Ha, H. T. 2022. Understanding the Institutional Challenge of Indo-Pacific Minilaterals to ASEAN. *Contemporary Southeast Asia, 44*(1), 1–30. https://www.jstor.org/stable/27130806

Le Hong, H. 2013. Vietnam's Hedging Strategy against China since Normalization. *Contemporary Southeast Asia, 35*(3), 333–368. Retrieved from http://www.jstor.org/stable/43281263

Thayer, C. A. 2018. The Evolution of Vietnamese Diplomacy, 1986–2016. In A. Tsvetov & H. H. Le (Eds.), *Vietnam's Foreign Policy under Doi Moi* (pp. 23–44): ISEAS–Yusof Ishak Institute.

Tran Viet Thai. 2015. Vietnamese foreign policy's strategic direction in the 21st century [Hướng đi chiến lược của ngoại giao Việt Nam trong thế kỷ 21]. *Vietnamese Government Newspaper*. https://baochinhphu.vn/huong-di-chien-luoc-cua-ngoai-giao-viet-nam-trong-the-ky-21-102195385.htm

Tuan, V. A. 2015. Ho Chi Minh thought on multilateralism [Tìm hiểu tư tưởng Hồ Chí Minh về ngoại giao đa phương]. *Thoi bao Quoc te [International Journal]*. https://tulieuvankien.dangcongsan. vn/c-mac-angghen-lenin-ho-chi-minh/ho-chi-minh/nghien-cuu-hoc-tap-tu-tuong/tim-hieu-tu-tuong-ho-chi-minh-ve-ngoai-giao-da-phuong-1986

Tung, N. V. 2021. *Flying Blind: Vietnam's Decision to Join ASEAN*: ISEAS-Yusof Ishak Institute.

Vietnam News Agency. 2015. Finland needs a neutral military foreign policy [Phần Lan cần chính sách ngoại giao trung lập về quân sự]. *Vietnam News Agency*. https://www.vietnamplus.vn/phan-lan-can-chinh-sach-ngoai-giao-trung-lap-ve-quan-su/318347.vnp

Vietnamese Communist Party. 2006. *Van kien Dang toan tap [Compilations of the Vietnamese Communist Party Documents] (1991)* (Vol. 51): National Political Publishing House.

Vu Khoan. 2015. Hồ Chí Minh - người đặt nền móng cho sự phát triển của nền ngoại giao cách mạng Việt Nam [Ho Chi Minh - who sets the foundation for the development of Vietnam's revolutionary diplomacy]. *Tap chi Quoc phong Toan dan [People's Defense Magazine]*. http://tapchiqptd.vn/vi/van-de-chung/ho-chi-minh-nguoi-dat-nen-mong-cho-su-phat-trien-cua-nen-ngoai-giao-cach-mang-viet-nam/7964.html

Vu, T. 2016. *Vietnam's Communist Revolution: The power and limits of ideology*. New York: Cambridge University Press.

6

Great Power Rivalry and Israeli Selective Neutrality: 'Walking Between the Drops'

LIUDMILA SAMARSKAIA

The concept of neutrality is not new in international relations, though its definition has always been situational. Israel, however, was never considered a neutral state during the Cold War period. It was involved in great power rivalry in the Middle East on the side of the West, most prominently the United States or France, in order to pursue its own security and policy goals. This alignment was more a function of the Soviet Union's support for Arab states, particularly Egypt and Syria. Israel's policies were always about Israeli security. The fall of the USSR, however, changed the strategic situation. Though the process of normalisation with Arab states began in the 1970s, the 1990s changed the balance of forces in the Middle East and gave temporary hope that the Arab-Israeli and Israeli-Palestinian conflicts could be resolved. While the latter remains unsettled, the former has been in many ways achieved. Such a realignment of forces changed the strategic positions of the State of Israel. This helped the Jewish state break international isolation and made cooperation with countries for which it used to be 'untouchable' possible.

While the US remains Israel's most important ally, Jerusalem has developed mutually beneficial relations with other important international players. For these parties, contacts with Israel usually fit into a wider strategy, and the once diminished importance of the Arab-Israeli conflict eventually served long-term foreign policy goals. The newly established (or resurrected) relations, however, have their issues and challenges. Despite the 'shadow' of the US and its security concerns – which proved decisive in certain cases – Israel's autonomy in its foreign policy choices remained significant, as it was in the Cold War. Therefore, it has continued to develop mutually beneficial contacts with all sides. At times, this resulted in Israel preserving a neutral stance even when the great power rivalry left few choices but to join one of the 'camps'. The 2022 Ukraine crisis became one of the latest examples of such positioning.

This chapter examines the historical roots of Israel's strategy towards the great powers, by briefly describing the Cold War period, then focusing on its aftermath in more detail – whilst analysing the role of neutrality. The study specifically focuses on the case of Israeli-Russian relations as the most illustrative in this respect, with Israeli-Chinese relations providing additional context. Principally, the analysis examines how the Israeli strategy of 'selective neutrality' manifested itself during the war in Ukraine.

The Foundations of Israeli Foreign Policy Strategy: The Great Power Factor

Just like the vast majority of the countries newly established as a result of the decolonisation process, Israel was haunted by the seemingly unavoidable task of choosing of a side at its inception, at the beginning of the Cold War. A tiny state in the midst of hostile neighbours, its foreign policy has always been closely intertwined with its security policy – the latter quite often substituting the former. In such circumstances, the attainment of short and long-term strategy goals turned out to be especially challenging. In the words of the first Israeli ambassador to the People's Republic of China, Zev Sufott (2000, 94), Israel's foreign policy in its early days 'was primarily focused on the need to obtain international recognition and material support in the face of hostility and boycott from its neighbours and in doing so had to seek help from greater powers to survive'.

Israel's first prime minister, David Ben-Gurion, (1966, 317) wrote that 'America's entry into the war made it clear that the decisive force when peace came would not be Britain but the United States'. Only the US 'had both the ability and the will to provide the massive economic aid that Israel required', which was demonstrated by a $100 million loan granted to Israel by the United States in 1949 (Telhami 1990, 403–404). Israel's early years as an independent state were characterised by the official politics of 'non-identification' – which it would have preferred to preserve but for the bipolar international system and the new great power rivalry unfolding in the Middle East as it became a frontier in the Cold War. A significant factor in that respect was the fact that the Jewish communities existed all over the world, both in socialist and in capitalist states, and Israel needed emigration channels open for all of them. Besides, many of the 'founding fathers' of Israel, including David Ben-Gurion, were socialists, and the first Israeli government had a left-wing majority (Zvyagelskaya 2012, 94).

It is possible to claim that initially Israel tried to pursue a 'small state' strategy. While it is questionable whether today's Israel can be considered a small state in terms of power, in 1948 it had to 'rely fundamentally on the aid of other states, institutions, processes, or developments' (Rothstein 1968, 29). Thus, it needed reliable partners with a vested interest in its survival while it simultaneously avoided antagonising other great powers. Even after decisively choosing a side during the Korean War in 1950, it still sought to maintain channels of communication with the Soviet Union. Besides, Israel sought to establish at least trade contacts with Beijing during the 1950s even though the US attitude towards that endeavour was, at times, quite adverse (Sufott 2000, 99–105).

Concurrently, Israel has pursued a strategy of self-reliance from its inception (Inbar and Sandler 1995, 45). An alliance with the US gave security benefits, including military and economic aid, but the US' withholding of arms transfers to Israel for several days during the Yom Kippur War of 1973 (Kober 2016, 210) confirmed the strategy of never fully relying on any one partner had proven wise. The alliance with the US remained crucial for successful deterrence of its adversaries, and therefore Israel had to take certain interests and concerns of Washington into consideration. Despite that, even during the Cold War, Jerusalem preferred to preserve its operational freedom and to hedge its risks. Consequently, its foreign policy was quite independent, largely characterised by self-reliance and constrained mainly by the logic of the Cold War confrontation.

Israeli Foreign Policy: A Multi-vector Approach

Israeli foreign policy after the end of the Cold War was in a way similar to the one it had been trying to pursue at the turn of 1940s–1950s. There was a range of new external and internal factors, however. The end of East-West politics brought a relief to tensions in the most contentious areas of the world, opened new ways for cooperation, but also gave rise to new challenges. There were crucial shifts in the strategic balance of power in the Middle East during the Gulf War of 1990–1991, principally via the weakening of Iraq. With the 'Arab threat' greatly diminished and Israeli military capacities significantly improved, Jerusalem's opportunities for successful manoeuvring were enhanced. Instead of a liability, being on good terms with Israel became a potential regional asset.

One of the main reasons for a change in attitude towards Israel on the international stage was the negotiations between Jerusalem and the Palestinians, first during the Madrid and the Moscow conferences in 1991 and 1992 and later in the course of the Oslo process, accompanied by Israeli-Palestinian mutual recognition and the conclusion of several relevant agreements. Despite the fact that the Oslo Accords did not eventually lead to a successful resolution of the Israel-Palestine conflict, they served as a demonstration of good intentions. A direct consequence was the establishment of official diplomatic relations between Jerusalem and a range of states – a leap forward in Israel's standing on the world stage. Regionally, the 1994 peace treaty with Jordan can be seen as the most significant development in this vein. African countries, which severed official relations with Israel after the 1973 Yom Kippur War, also embarked upon a process of gradual restoration. As Efraim Inbar (2020, 244) puts it, 'for Israel, the upgrading of relations with Russia, India, China, Turkey, (and) Nigeria ... was an end to its relative international isolation'.

While Israel was enthusiastic about new partnerships in the 1990s, their significance has only increased gradually. There were several factors that influenced the further development of the multi-vector approach in Israeli foreign politics. The start of the United States' gradual withdrawal from the Middle East beginning in 2009 demonstrated that the region was no longer as central for Washington. This, coupled with disagreements between US president, Barack Obama, and Israeli prime minister, Benjamin Netanyahu, on the Israeli-Palestinian conflict resolution, led Israel to the conclusion that it needed to further diversify its international relations. Besides, developing relations with other significant extra-regional powers like Russia and China demonstrated that Jerusalem had 'other options' and wasn't overly dependent on Washington. This served as a continuation of Israel's previous policy of self-reliance, the relevance of which has never disappeared. Benjamin Netanyahu, Israel's longest-serving prime minister, wrote the following:

> Nothing could replace our indispensable alliance with the United States, a partnership rooted in common civilizational values. But this did not mean that the United States should be our *only* ally. Thus, in my first term, I sought to warm ties between Israel and two other global powers, China and Russia (Netanyahu 2022, 270).

A feature of Netanyahu's approach frequently exercised with regard to other world powers is its occasionally demonstrative nature. One example of such positioning took place in 2023. While Netanyahu has not been invited to the White House since his re-election in late-2022, he informed the members of a US Congressional delegation during a meeting in June 2023 that he had received an invitation to visit China, which would be his fourth trip there (Prime Minister's Office 2023). Though probably done as part of the aforementioned strategy to show that Israel had 'other options', the real effect of this gesture was questioned even by Israeli experts who warned against antagonising the US – especially in the context of strained relations because of Israel's right-wing coalition government (Inbar 2023).

Going back to the Obama era, a serious bone of contention between Israel and the US during the Obama administration was the Joint Comprehensive

Plan of Action (JCPOA), or the Iran nuclear deal, which Israel vehemently opposed. While the relevance of the Israeli-Palestinian conflict was gradually diminishing for Jerusalem at this time, the importance of the 'Iranian issue' was progressively growing. The Iranian nuclear program and the risks its further development entailed for Israel have been attracting the limelight of its foreign and security politics since the 1990s. In that context, the development of relations with countries that could have leverage on Tehran turned into a strategic asset. That way, Israel could inform both Moscow and Beijing of its concerns. Israeli-American ties endured despite the political contradictions and strained personal relations between Netanyahu and Obama. In 2016, Obama signed a 10-year Memorandum of Understanding for 2018–2028, which became 'the largest single pledge of military assistance in U.S. history', totalling $38 billion. This demonstrated the strategic character of bilateral relations and the US' profound commitment to Israeli security (Fact Sheet: Memorandum of Understanding Reached with Israel 2016).

Returning to the present, one of the most illustrative examples in this respect was the quick US reaction to the October 2023 Israel-Gaza war, which started with a brutal Hamas attack against Israel and which involves risks of a broader regional escalation involving Hezbollah and Iran (among others). US aircraft carriers, which Washington sent to the Eastern Mediterranean, were meant to serve as deterrents against any further anti-Israeli actions by Tehran and its proxies (Lamothe and Sands 2023). The reasons for such US policy lie in ideological considerations (supporting Israel as 'the only democracy in the Middle East' and as the nation-state of the Jewish people), though strategic calculations (common security/threat perceptions) also play their part (Weinberg 2014, 63–65). There is also the factor of American domestic politics, which manifests itself most starkly during election campaigns. The Jewish community, which also has a network of lobbying organisations, and evangelical Christians, who tend to be favourable towards Israel, are influential electoral groups – with the latter comprising around a quarter of the US population.

Israeli foreign policy is focused on preserving the Jewish state and encouraging Jewish immigration to their 'national home'. In all other respects, Jerusalem's foreign policy is profoundly pragmatic and non-ideological – especially when compared to the American and European approach. For Israel, the government system that exists in a partner state is of no relevance and remains as was formulated during the Cold War in the 1969 Basic Foreign Principles of the Government of Israel:

> The Government will continue to work for the establishment of friendly ties and mutual relations between Israel and all peace-loving States, irrespective of their internal regime, and without injuring the interests of other nations.

Likewise for Russia and China, promoting a certain ideology has not been central for their foreign policy since the end of the Cold War. Their interest towards the Middle East was dictated by security and economic considerations. In that respect, Israel was treated as a key player and one of the most promising partners in the region, with its highly developed military technologies, strong tech sector, and a vibrant economy. For many of the newer Israeli partners, relations with Jerusalem were also one of the potential ways to 'pave the road' to Washington – either to gain an additional channel of communication or to curry favour with one of the most influential international players (Inbar 2020, 243–244). One of the most recent examples of such an approach was the case of Sudan which was removed from America's State Sponsor of Terrorism list as part of, reportedly, an Israeli-Sudanese normalisation deal signed in 2021 (Zaidan 2023). Hence, beside economic and technological benefits, cooperation with Jerusalem can potentially bring strategic dividends.

One reason for Israel's successful manoeuvring lies in the fact that it doesn't have any vital strategic contradictions with extra-regional actors. The Israeli-Palestinian conflict is certainly a contentious issue, but an agreed solution is not always a top priority even on the US agenda, let alone other great powers. The only significant exception in this respect is the EU, and this has affected the otherwise productive Israeli-European relationship. There's also the topic of the Iranian nuclear program, nowadays central for the Israeli rhetoric, which also draws significant criticism from the world community because of its potential military aspects. Other than that, there are no real foundations for significant rivalry with Israel, as the main goal of Israeli foreign policy (the preservation of its security) is not questioned by any major external power.

During the post-Cold War period, Israel's strategic positions have gradually improved. The Arab-Israeli conflict (Israel's historic conflicts and disputes with Egypt, Jordan, and other Arab neighbours) has all but disappeared from the international agenda, while its Israeli-Palestinian component has been largely deprioritised by most regional players (at least before 7 October). Meanwhile, countering the 'Iranian threat' has taken a central place in Jerusalem's foreign policy strategy, a concern it shares with the bulk of Arab states. In these conditions, Israel, witnessing a gradual diminishing of the US interest in the region, started forging new partnerships aimed at strengthening its strategic positions. Israel's self-positioning became in many ways unique. Nowadays, Jerusalem is not only a major US non-NATO ally, but also a state that has a 'special relationship' with Washington. Historically, Israel has been the leading recipient of American military aid (Davydov and Samarskaia 2020). In addition, Israel enjoys thriving economic relations with China and a mutually suitable partnership with Russia, both of which are perceived as key strategic adversaries of the US. Despite superficial similarities between Israeli-Chinese and Israeli-Russian relations, they differ in significant ways. Each have their specific traits, determined by the history of their development and the character of these two states' interests in the region.

Russia: Security First

Israeli relations with Russia, and earlier with the Soviet Union, have always been complicated. On the one hand, the USSR supported the partition of Palestine in 1947 – which eventually led to the creation of Israel. The Soviet Union was the first country to recognise Israel both *de jure* and *de facto* in 1948 – while the US at first recognised Israel *de facto* only, withholding *de jure* recognition until 1949. The USSR was also behind the significant arms supplies to Israel (transferred by Czechoslovakia and through Yugoslavia) before and during Israel's War of Independence 1948–1949, which played a crucial role in Israel's military successes and its very survival. While the Soviet government had its own pragmatic considerations in making these decisions, namely to weaken British influence in the Middle East (Kober 2016, 209), Israel has never forgotten these important gestures.

On the other hand, the logic of the Cold War placed Israel and the USSR on opposite sides. This became quite evident by the early 1950s, when Israel supported the UN resolution condemning North Korea's invasion of South Korea. Relations then worsened in 1967 when bilateral diplomatic relations were severed as a result of the Six-Day War, as the USSR had armed and assisted the Arab states that had attacked Israel – principally Egypt. There was also the issue of Jewish emigration, which the Soviet Union vehemently opposed for ideological reasons, and the problem of Soviet state-supported antisemitism, which reached its peak at the beginning of the 1950s with the Slansky trial (1952) and the 'doctors' plot' affair (1951–1953) (Nosenko and Semenchenko 2015, 22), but transformed later into intense anti-Zionism.

The situation changed with the launch of reforms in the USSR in the 1980s, accompanied by gradual liberalisation, which led to an opening of the gates to emigration for Soviet Jewry. Israel's official diplomatic relations with the Soviet Union were restored at the very end of the Cold War period, in 1991, and Israeli-Russian ties became their logical continuation. The substantial upgrading of relations was not immediate. After initial enthusiasm, by the middle of the 1990s the rapprochement somewhat slowed down. The first Russian (and the last Soviet) ambassador to Israel, Aleksandr Bovin, despite being generally optimistic of further positive shifts in contacts, explained it in the following way in 1994:

> The reasons [were] twofold. On the Russian side – the general instability of the situation, conflicts in the 'near abroad', the inertia of the pro-Arab tradition. On the Israeli side – mistrust

inherited from a quarter-century long period of hostility, fear of Russia sliding back to pro-imperial, right-wing nationalist positions (Bovin 2001, 407).

Despite such challenges, cooperation agreements were signed in various spheres, including trade, security, technology, agriculture, and tourism. Further steps were taken later under improved personal relations under the premiership of Ariel Sharon and presidency of Vladimir Putin at the turn of 2000s (Rumer 2019, 12–13). In this period, one of the factors that brought Israel and Russia together was a common perception of Islamist terrorism as a foremost security threat. An example of that was the fact that Jerusalem did not criticise Moscow on its Chechnya military campaign, in contrast with a vast majority of Western countries. During his second period as prime minister (2009–21), Netanyahu's personal relations with Putin preserved the prior momentum. As a sign of symbolically 'special' relations between Israel and Russia, Netanyahu was one of the few foreign leaders to be invited to Moscow in 2018 for the 9 May Victory Day celebrations. This emphasised the factor of collective memory in bilateral ties. The Israeli and Russian approaches to the historical memory of World War Two are in many ways similar – and that is appreciated by both sides (Aharonson 2018).

Relations in this period have not always been smooth. After the Russo-Georgian conflict in 2008, during which Moscow accused Jerusalem of providing military aid to Tbilisi, Israel has been careful to not antagonise Russia on such issues. Additionally, in 2010, a five-year military agreement was signed which included Israeli UAV sales to Moscow and even setting up joint drone production on Russian territory (Hilsman 2015). Whilst this initiative made an important contribution to the Russian UAV industry, it was later curbed because of American concerns and Israeli fears of potential technology transfers to Iran and its regional proxies. Economic relations between the countries have also been unremarkable. In 2022, total trade volume barely exceeded $1 billion, with Russia only being in the top twenty of Israel's trade partners in Europe (Israel's Foreign Trade in Goods, by Country, June 2023). Israel, on the other hand, was one of the top ten trade partners for Russia in the MENA region in 2021 (Russia Exports by Country 2023; Russia Imports by Country 2023).

In the broader sense, post-Cold War relations with Russia have had a strategic significance for Israel for two reasons. On the one hand, Russia's balancing politics in the Middle East allows it to maintain contacts with all the key powers in the region – which makes Moscow a potentially valuable mediator. Additionally, in several cases, direct Israeli-Russian dialogue helped postpone or cancel Russian arms sales to Iran or Syria. Russia's presence in Syria since 2015 (following its civil war and the rise of Islamic State) also made it Israel's 'northern neighbour', which presented both challenges and new opportunities.

As Syrian territory was used by Iranian proxies, Israel needed significant freedom of action in the Syrian sky to prevent unwanted arms transfers or establishments of terrorist military bases in proximity to its territory. This led to the setting up of an Israeli-Russian deconfliction mechanism which effectively forestalled cases of 'friendly fire' and a deep Iranian entrenchment on Syrian territory, which was undesirable for both sides. That way, while Russia served as a balancing factor against Iran for Israel – Israel played the same role for Russia, which has not been eager to share its sphere of influence with Tehran (Rumer 2019, 15–16).

An additional challenge for bilateral relations arose during the October 2023 Israel-Gaza war, the consequences of which are still unfolding. The Russian stance on the 7 October Hamas attack initially proved to be much less critical than what could have been expected in case of such a serious act of terror, especially considering Russia's recent history of combating terrorism. The invitation of Hamas leaders to Moscow just weeks after the start of hostilities became an additional cause for Russian-Israeli tensions. While the calls for a ceasefire and negotiations to reach the two-state solution have always been an integral part of Moscow's position during such escalations, the criticism of Israel's actions and the US' policies in the MENA in general was exceptionally intense (Osborn 2023).

At the same time, harsh Russian rhetoric in this case can be perceived more as a consequence of its wider confrontation with Western countries, the US in particular, due to the war in Ukraine, rather than specific enmity towards Israel. In a way, that partially resembled the Soviet attitude towards Israel, with the USSR not wishing Israel's destruction and being mainly concerned with great power rivalry. Despite this new public stance, which is highly critical of Israeli actions in Gaza, there are no signs of Russia's practical involvement on Hamas' side. In that respect, Moscow's position on the Israel-Hamas escalation seems in a way similar to Jerusalem's attitude towards the Russia-Ukraine conflict, which will be discussed later in this chapter. While Israel reciprocated by voicing stronger criticism of Russia's contacts with Hamas and closer interaction with Iran, it has nevertheless not taken any concrete confrontational steps (Erlanger and Sella 2024). Therefore, for now, it is possible to assume that the influence of the 2023 Israel-Gaza war on Russian-Israeli relations may not be as significant as current rhetoric might suggest.

The case of Russian-Israeli relations is in many ways unique. One of the main reasons for this is the large Russian-speaking population of Israel. During the perestroika period, hundreds of thousands of Soviet Jews emigrated to Israel. They formed a large Russian-speaking community, which at one time amounted to nearly 20 per cent of the Israeli population – becoming an important factor in Russian-Israeli relations. In a 2022 poll, Russia was named the most important country for Israel (not considering the US) by 40 per cent of the population (The Israeli Foreign Policy Index 2022). The dynamics of Israelis' attitude towards Russia, however, demonstrates a decisive downward trend: while in 2019 the percentage of Israelis who viewed it favourably reached 45 per cent (a high point during the last 15 years), by 2023, as a consequence of the war in Ukraine, it had plummeted to 13 per cent (Fagan et al. 2023). This marks the reality that Israeli-Russian relations have passed through different periods: From the 'honeymoon' at the end of the 1940s, through ideological confrontation from the 1950s until the 1980s, and to pragmatic and productive ties after the end of the Cold War. While technically both are aligned with mutually antagonistic powers (the US and Iran respectively), they manage to maintain constructive dialogue which is beneficial for both sides, despite the curbing of cooperation in sensitive military spheres. Israeli-Russian ties are in many ways guided by their own logic which is based on special pages in their history, ongoing cultural and social contacts, strategic considerations, and, perhaps most importantly, a similar perception of security threats. This all makes both sides susceptible to their respective concerns. This makes the Israeli choice of neutrality in certain cases quite natural, and its position with regard to the war in Ukraine is the most illustrative in this respect.

The War in Ukraine

One of the starkest examples of Israel's politics of neutrality has been its position on the war in Ukraine, which started in February 2022 with Russia's 'special military operation'. While voicing opposition to Russia's invasion, supplying humanitarian aid to Ukraine and hosting thousands of fleeing Ukrainians, Israel has refrained from joining Western countries in imposing sanctions on Russia (just like it did after the annexation of Crimea in 2014), has avoided supplying any offensive weapons to Ukraine, and has maintained dialogue with both sides. Despite internal and external criticism (Shavit et al. 2022), Jerusalem's stance hasn't significantly changed since February 2022. The most it has done was arrange to set up an early warning system against missile attacks in Ukraine and, most recently, electronic warfare systems defending against drone attacks (Times of Israel staff 2023).

Another feature of (and justification for) Israel's neutral stance was an attempt by then-prime minister Naftali Bennett to serve as mediator between the sides. Bennett, being an Orthodox Jew, flew to Moscow on Shabbat – thus breaking it, which, according to Halakha (the Jewish law), is allowed only if it can save a human life (Zilber 2022). The attempt proved futile, though it highlighted Israel's possible capacity to be an actor able and willing to talk directly to both sides. In that respect, Israel's behaviour was similar to that of several other Middle Eastern states (such as Turkey, Saudi Arabia, and UAE), Asian states (such as China, India), Latin American states (such as Brazil), and African states (such as South Africa), which can be broadly described as representing 'the Global South' and which also took a neutral position on the Russia-Ukraine conflict while trying to resolve it through diplomatic means.

The main reasons Israel cites to justify its neutral stance with regard to the conflict are again derived from security concerns. First, it strives to preserve its relative freedom of action over Syria. Second, it is not ready to risk its arms and weaponry falling into the hands of Iran and its proxies (whether through Russia or any other way). Finally, it has to worry about the fate of the Jewish community in Russia which, while not directly threatened, still remains vulnerable to any deterioration of bilateral ties. The latter was demonstrated when, in the summer of 2022, a case was opened against the Russian branch of the Jewish Agency (Sokhnut), which works on Jewish immigration to Israel. The Russian Ministry of Justice demanded the Sokhnut's closure because of personal data collection breaches (Gross 2022). This further underlined the need to preserve direct channels of bilateral contacts which could defuse any arising tensions.

Even in the joint US-Israel Strategic Partnership Declaration signed in Jerusalem on 14 July 2022 during President Biden's visit to the Middle East, the wording concerning the war in Ukraine was cautious and obscure. No mention of Russia was made and no direct accusations were voiced:

> The United States and Israel reiterate their concerns regarding the ongoing attacks against Ukraine, their commitment to Ukraine's sovereignty and territorial integrity, and affirmed the importance of continued humanitarian assistance to the people of Ukraine (The Jerusalem U.S.-Israel Strategic Partnership Joint Declaration 2022).

Closer Russian-Iranian cooperation since 2022 has not significantly changed the Israeli position for several possible reasons. Because of the factors listed above, Russia probably has more leverage over Israel than the reverse. Therefore, confrontation with Moscow could be detrimental to Israeli security. Additionally, Israel's decisive practical alignment with Ukraine could well lessen the incentive for Russia to stay neutral in the Israel–Iran relationship in the Middle East, thus strengthening Tehran's position.

The war in Ukraine starkly demonstrated that Israel's politics of 'selective neutrality' does not depend on domestic politics. While the public rhetoric varied from one prime minister to the other and from minister of foreign affairs to his successor, a constant political and strategic line has been preserved. Despite condemning Russian actions, most Israeli citizens approve of the more or less neutral stance of the Israeli government. In a poll conducted in 2022, 53 per cent of the respondents agreed with the government's policy of 'walking between the drops', while 28 per cent expressed full support of 'Ukraine and the position of the liberal-democratic world', with only two per cent fully siding with Russia (The Israeli Foreign Policy Index 2022). In another poll, also conducted in 2022, 60 per cent agreed that Israel's decision to refrain from imposing sanctions on Russia was correct, with 68 per cent claiming that Israel should not supply Ukraine with military equipment (Hermann et al. 2022).

Israel's positioning in the context of the war in Ukraine was in many ways a logical continuation of its previous politics towards the great powers, and towards Russia in particular. The 'selective neutrality', or 'walking between the drops', or 'sitting on the fence', was a strategic choice motivated largely by security considerations. The US pressure in this case evidently turned out to be relatively minor, with Washington likely respecting Israel's concerns, allowing Jerusalem a greater level of flexibility to reflect its unique security needs.

Conclusion

Since its inception, Israel has had to seek the support of greater powers. The reliance on external forces, however, has never been complete. Just as the British were only temporary allies in Israel's formative years, Jerusalem, while fully appreciating the 'special relationship' it enjoys with Washington, still prefers to preserve a wide policy space and to manoeuvre accordingly. With Israel, neutrality – or rather, a multi-vector approach – has served as a successful strategy during the post-Cold War period. While relations with the United States have remained of vital importance for both sides, with chances for a significant reconfiguration remaining relatively low, Israel's ties with Russia and China have also developed extensively. Even as Israeli-Russian and Israeli-Chinese developments in the military sphere were mostly curbed by the beginning of the 2020s, economic relations continued, security contacts intensified (mostly with Russia due to its presence in Syria), and cultural and educational programs widened. As the war in Ukraine has unfolded, Russian-Israeli relations have become somewhat frozen, though both sides have an interest in their preservation and have navigated comparably difficult waters in the past. On the whole, the Israeli strategy of neutrality is part of a wider strategy of maintaining productive relations with the world's greater powers, deriving from the perception of a constant existential threat that haunted Israel since its inception – and continues to this day.

References

Aharonson, Micky. 2018. "Relations between Israel and the USSR/Russia". The Jerusalem Institute for Strategy and Security, May 1. https://jiss.org.il/en/aharonson-relations-israel-ussr-russia/

Ben-Gurion, David, ed. 1966. *The Jews in their Land*. London: Aldus Books Limited.

Telhami, Shibley. "Israeli Foreign Policy: A Static Strategy in a Changing World". *Middle East Journal* 44, no. 3 (Summer 1990): 399–416.

Bovin, Aleksandr. 2001. *Notes from a Non-Professional Ambassador*. Moscow: Zacharov Publishing House.

Cohen, Stuart A. 2012. "Light and Shadows in US-Israeli Military Ties, 1948–2010". In *Israel and the United States: Six Decades of US–Israeli Relations*, edited by Robert Owen Freedman, 143–164. Boulder: Westview Press.

Davydov, Alexey and Liudmila Samarskaia. 2020. "The U.S.-Israel "Special Relations": Structural Foundations and Trump Factor". *World Economy and International Relations*, 64, no. 10: 40–51. https://doi.org/10.20542/0131-2227-2020-64-10-40-51

Duhamel, Constantin. 2022. "Russia – Israel Trade and Investment 2022". Russia Briefing, August 31. https://www.russia-briefing.com/news/russia-israel-trade-and-investment-2022.html/

Erlanger, Steven and Adam Sella. 2024. "Israel Faces Tough Balancing Act on Russia and the West". *The New York Times*, March 19. https://www.nytimes.com/2024/03/19/world/europe/israel-russia-us-ukraine.html

Fagan, Moira, Jacob Poushter and Sneha Gubbala. 2023. "Large Shares See Russia and Putin in Negative Light, While Views of Zelenskyy More Mixed". Pew Research Center, July 10. https://www.pewresearch.org/global/2023/07/10/overall-opinion-of-russia/

Hermann, Tamar, Or Anabi, Yaron Kaplan, Inna Orly Sapozhnikova. 2022. "60% of Israelis Back the Government's Policy on the Russia-Ukraine Conflict — Special Survey". The Israel Democracy Institute, March 5. https://en.idi.org.il/articles/38624

Hilsman, Patrick. 2015. "Analysis: Drone deals heighten military ties between Israel and Russia". Middle East Eye, October 4. https://www.middleeasteye. net/news/analysis-drone-deals-heighten-military-ties-between-israel-and-russia

Inbar, Efraim. 2020. "Israel's Pivot from Europe to Asia". In *Israel Under Netanyahu: Domestic Politics and Foreign Policy*, edited by Robert Owen Freedman. 242–261. Abingdon / New York: Routledge.

Inbar, Efraim. 2023. "Should Netanyahu go to China?" The Jerusalem Institute for Strategy and Security, July 20. https://jiss.org.il/en/inbar-should-netanyahu-go-to-china/

Inbar, Efraim and Shmuel Sandler. 1995 "The Changing Israeli Strategic Equation: Toward a Security Regime". *Review of International Studies.* 21, no. 1: 41–59.

"Israel's Foreign Trade in Goods, by Country — June 2023". Central Bureau of Statistics, July 24. https://www.cbs.gov.il/en/mediarelease/pages/2023/israel's-foreign-trade-in-goods,-by-country-june-2023.aspx

Gross, Judah Ari. 2022. "Jewish Agency trial in Moscow postponed again, leaving group's fate unclear". The Times of Israel, September 19. https://www.timesofisrael.com/jewish-agency-trial-in-moscow-postponed-again-leaving-groups-fate-unclear/

Kober, Avi. 2016. "Arms Races and the Arab–Israeli Conflict". In *Arms Races in International Politics: From the Nineteenth to the Twenty-First Century*, edited by Thomas Mahnken, Joseph Maiolo, and David Stevenson, 205–223. Oxford: Oxford University Press.

Lamothe, Dan and Leo Sands. 2023. "Pentagon surging thousands of troops toward Israel amid Gaza war". The Washington Post, October 17. https://www.washingtonpost.com/world/2023/10/17/us-deploys-sailors-marines-israel-hamas/

Ministry of Foreign Affairs (Israel). 1969. "Basic Foreign Policy Principles of the Government of Israel". December 15. https://www.gov.il/en/Departments/General/11-basic-foreign-policy-principles-of-the-government-of-israel-15-december-1969

Netanyahu, Benjamin. 2022. *Bibi: My Story*. New York / London: Threshold Editions.

Nosenko, Tatiana and Nina Semenchenko. 2015. *The Vain Enmity: Essays of the Soviet-Israeli Relations 1948–1991*. Moscow: IV RAN.

Osborn, Andrew. 2023 "Russia's Putin tries to use Gaza war to his geopolitical advantage". Reuters, November 17. https://www.reuters.com/world/russias-putin-sees-political-economic-upside-israels-war-with-hamas-2023-11-17/

Rothstein, Robert. *Alliances and Small Powers*. New York: Columbia University Press, 1968.

Rumer, Eugene. 2019. *Russia in the Middle East: Jack of All Trades, Master of None*. Washington: Carnegie Endowment for International Peace.

"Russia imports by country," Trading Economics, accessed August 8, 2023. https://tradingeconomics.com/russia/imports-by-country

Shavit, Eldad, Udi Dekel and Anat Kurz. 2022. "The Cold War is Heating Up: Implications for Israel". Special Publication, The Institute for National Security Studies, February 23. https://www.inss.org.il/publication/russia-usa-tenion/

Sufott, Zev. 2000. "Israel's China Policy 1950–92". *Israel Affairs*. 7, no. 1: 94–118. http://dx.doi.org/10.1080/13537120008719591

Times of Israel staff. 2023. "In first, Israel said to authorize sale of defensive military equipment to Ukraine". March 16. https://www.timesofisrael.com/in-first-israel-said-to-authorize-sale-of-defensive-military-equipment-to-ukraine/

"The Israeli Foreign Policy Index of 2022". The Israeli Institute for Regional Foreign Policies, October. https://mitvim.org.il/en/publication/the-israeli-foreign-policy-index-of-2022/

The White House. 2016. "Fact Sheet: Memorandum of Understanding Reached with Israel,". President Barack Obama, September 14. https://obamawhitehouse.archives.gov/the-press-office/2016/09/14/fact-sheet-memorandum-understanding-reached-israel

The White House. 2022. "The Jerusalem U.S.-Israel Strategic Partnership Joint Declaration,", July 14. https://www.whitehouse.gov/briefing-room/statements-releases/2022/07/14/the-jerusalem-u-s-israel-strategic-partnership-joint-declaration/

Weinberg, David Andrew. 2014. "Israel and the United States: An Alliance Like No Other". In *Israel and the World Powers: Diplomatic Alliances and International Relations beyond the Middle East*. edited by Colin Schindler, 61–91. London: I.B. Tauris.

Zaidan, Yasir. 2023. "The Sudan-Israel normalization process: A tactical move but a strategic hazard". Stroum Center for Jewish Studies, University of Washington, May 22. https://jewishstudies.washington.edu/israel-hebrew/sudan-israel-normalization-diplomatic-relations-netanyahu-al-burhan/

Zilber, Neri. 2022. "Why Naftali Bennett Went to Moscow". *Foreign Policy*, March 7. https://foreignpolicy.com/2022/03/07/israel-ukraine-mediation-russia-bennett-putin/

7

Oman: Partisan Non-Intervention

ROBY C. BARRETT AND LEAH SHERWOOD

Since the end of the Cold War, foreign policy experts have often labelled Oman as neutral. While Oman often adopts non-interventionist positions, it is an oversimplification to call Muscat neutral. Indeed, the notion fails to capture the complexity of Oman's policies and the tangled internal historical experience that informs its foreign relations. Contemporary Omani policy results from Sultan Qaboos bin Said Al Bu Said's (who ruled from 1970–2020) perceptions of regime vulnerabilities in the sultanate's post-independence era. These perceptions are a direct product of Oman's past and, if the present under Sultan Haitham bin Tarik (who has ruled from 2020–present) is a measure, they will continue to provide the guiding principles for the future. Oman's external behaviour cannot be described as neutrality, as Oman has used non-aligned or non-interventionist policies as a tactical façade since the 1980s. It does this to manage conflicts and relationships that could pose a threat to the Al Bu Said regime or Oman's territorial integrity, all the while being fully aware that its existential, strategic security is inextricably linked to its relationship with the West and the United States (US).

If not neutral, then how should we define Omani foreign and security policy? For the purposes of this effort, the term 'partisan non-intervention' provides a useful umbrella for discussing not only Oman's contemporary security behaviour, but also the internal and external perceptions from which it flows. Oman's partisan non-intervention is best described in three parts. First, an explanation of contemporary policy highlights the duality of Al Bu Said's policies since 1991. Far from any ideological attachment to the norms underscoring neutrality, such as a foreign policy commitment to not taking sides, Oman's position on any given regional or international issue is first and foremost partisan and at times disconnected from the preferences of Oman's erstwhile partners in the Gulf Cooperation Council (GCC). These policies also provide a degree of separation from US official policy as well. Instead, the Omani regime perceives these policies as supporting its own interests, namely the preservation of the Al Bu Said dynasty, and the territorial integrity of the Omani state. Non-intervention also allows Oman to play a niche role as a conduit for diplomatic dialogue. Non-intervention is not a doctrinaire commitment on Oman's part; it is realpolitik, and as such does not preclude self-interest-based confrontation or intervention. Thus, Omani non-intervention is situational and as such can be best understood through an examination of its unique historical context, and state formation process.

Secondly, at a fundamental level, the tribal, sectarian, and geographical realities of Oman created a challenging tableau for its state creation and stability. What the Al Bu Said, and more specifically Sultan Qaboos, faced in 1970 was nothing less than new state formation – prior to that, the British dominated and defined the Sultanate's options within the British imperial context. Qaboos not only inherited the domestic problems that intensified during his father's rule, but also the handicaps bequeathed to the Muscat regime by British colonial policy and the dynastic Arab rivalries across the region. Due to regional and internal political fragility, and recognizing the limitations of Oman's small state reality, Qaboos formulated security relationships that protected the integrity of the state and safeguarded the Al Bu Said dynasty. This reality, combined with the historical experience dominated by the British imperial system, illuminates the present, and provides an informed glimpse into its future, foreign policy. In short, the complexities of Oman's policies of pragmatic non-intervention are coupled with the fractious givens of the geopolitical and socio-cultural environment, the ongoing challenges of state formation, and the exceptionalist nature of Sultan Qaboos' rule. The future will likely be awash in political, economic, socio-cultural, and security challenges, and attempts to renationalize the succession process may or may not prove to be a stabilizing factor. These complications constitute a looming challenge for changes in the application of pragmatic non-intervention.

Modern Oman: Self-Interest and Non-Intervention

Three critical factors shape Oman's interlinked foreign and domestic policies: (1) its strategic location, (2) its modern adaptation of Ibadi "conservatism and tolerance," and (3) its fractured ethnic, sectarian, and tribal identity. These factors explain Oman's preference for balancing policies of non-intervention and compromise regarding regional and international issues. To offer a more nuanced analysis, this section examines Omani policy from 1991 to 2020 and addresses the problematic use of the word 'neutral', when, in fact, Oman is decidedly partisan in its policy preferences. Oman recognizes there is no replacement for its strategic alliance with the US and the West. Given its own history of conflict resulting from foreign interventions inside Oman, Muscat is highly attuned to the pitfalls of poorly conceived intervention. Oman only acts when threats to its dynastic and/or state survival exist, basing its fundamental policies on an independent and reliably pragmatic national security approach rooted in the logic of prioritising the *longue durée* over open-ended and even petty quarrels.

Partisan Non-Intervention and Situational Neutrality in Contemporary Policy

Oman's 'partisan non-intervention', or 'situational neutrality', is not *de jure* neutrality. In fact, Oman pursues an alliance-based security strategy, and has since the late 1700s. However, while allying with Britain for 200 years ensured the survival of the Al Bu Said regime, it also brought the loss of Muscat's political independence. Lacking 'hard power', Oman still has to rely on more powerful allies for its ultimate security today. However, since independence in 1970, Muscat has not only focused on retaining the benefits of an alliance-based security, but has worked to curb its impact on its political autonomy. In this regard, Muscat utilises soft power, which often gives the illusion of neutrality. For example, during the Cold War, despite declaring its non-alignment, Oman launched cross-border raids into Yemen and relied on Western support to fight a bitter war against a Soviet and Chinese-sponsored insurgency (Gunther 2020; Tètreault 1991, 567). Upon closer inspection, Oman's membership in the Non-Aligned Movement shielded it from some political consequences related to its Western alignment at a time of rising Arab nationalism (Casey 2007, 12; Kochan 1972, 508–510). Another tactic is for Oman to differentiate between politics and ideology. In Arabic, the equivalent of 'non-alignment' is commonly translated as *hiyad al-ijabi* meaning 'positive neutralism' (Agwani 1981, 371). Officially, this means that Muscat conducts relations 'without reference to position' to deprioritise politico-military affiliations and ideological positions (Sayegh 1964, 64). This translates into a series of situational positions on sensitive topics keyed to the prioritisation of Omani interests. The ongoing Iran-UAE territorial dispute is one example. Oman's Ministry of Foreign Affairs states, 'the current dispute between the UAE and Iran over Abu Musa and the Tunbs should not be allowed to impede the continuing development of Omani–Iranian relations' (Jones and Ridout 2012, 158). Oman is not neutral on the issue of the islands, but rather sees nothing to be gained given its perceived *fait accompli,* and Oman's desire to maintain diverse cooperative relationships, especially with Tehran.

In this regard, Oman has negotiated security arrangements with various regional and international powers, and yet Oman's relationship with the US, which includes bases, joint operations, security cooperation, remains the backbone of Muscat's defence policy (US Department of State, POLMIL, June 15, 2021). The other arrangements mostly pertain to limited intelligence sharing, training, and facility access to advance regional security cooperation. (Cafiero 2016,

49–55). This diversification is a method to hedge against over-reliance on any one partner, while simultaneously building political bridges that let it better negotiate the boundaries of its power to pursue its own interests. Another tool Oman also uses to offset the constraints an alliance-based security imposes is by using its constitution to limit the use of force, which enables it to avoid military interventions (Cafiero and Karasik 2017a).

Oman attempts to project the image of itself as a 'helper' whose 'good offices' are useful during mediation of regional conflicts. This distinction between support and neutral non-involvement is key, and it distinguishes Oman from those that aspire to a more doctrinaire neutralist stance. In 2003, the Omani Foreign Minister explained, 'we have room for maneuver that the big states themselves do not enjoy. We can operate without attracting too much attention, conduct diplomacy discreetly and quietly' (Badr Al Bu Said, 2003). Under Qaboos, Oman's foreign policy was thus infused with his adaption of Ibadi principles, stressing dialogue, tolerance, unity, cooperation, and diplomacy (Sherwood 2017a, 11). This pragmatic use of soft power to offset potential threats has proven to be effective. At times, it has increased Oman's influence, moderated pressures on Muscat extending from Gulf political discourse, and improved regional security cooperation while obfuscating Oman's dependence on Western security guarantees for its strategic survival to some degree.

Non-intervention and the Complexity in Intra-GCC Relations

Although the GCC states share common security challenges, mutual distrust and suspicion impede strong levels of intra-GCC strategic cooperation. This is hardly surprising given that the dynasties have in fact been often bitter rivals at one time or another since the eighteenth century. From the Omani perspective, the GCC states have been ineffective in defending GCC interests, and, more importantly, they have often represented greater threats to Oman than Iran. These Arab threats to Oman's sovereignty, and Muscat's recognition that GCC states' threat perceptions and interests frequently differ, made Muscat leery of greater GCC political and military integration. This aversion to integration has manifested itself in several ways. Much to the chagrin of Riyadh and Abu Dhabi, Oman made it clear that it would 'not be part of' a military alliance that was primarily anti-Iranian in nature. Bin Alawi expressed Oman's expectations of a Western security umbrella: 'It is a Western responsibility [*to provide security*] because they have their [*oil*] interests here [...]' (Hamidaddin 2013). Oman's approach is to work with major powers, and to try to stay on the sidelines as much as possible in the context of GCC political and security conflicts by offering to play constructive roles such as providing conflict resolution services.

In 2011, Qaboos refused to participate in the Arab Spring effort by Riyadh and Abu Dhabi to quash the Shi'a rebellion in Bahrain. Muscat argued that the Al

Khalifah should treat the Shi'a with respect, as they are Bahraini citizens, and the regime should find a political situation based on compromise. He likewise refused to support their 2015 intervention in Yemen against the Houthi-backed regime in Sanaa (Neubauer 2016a; Chatham House 2015). When a Saudi-led military intervention in Yemen occurred, Oman declared its neutrality and offered diplomatic good offices (Cafiero 2015a). Qaboos hosted a meeting between Iran's Foreign Minister, Javad Zarif, and Houthi, Saudi, and US representatives in Muscat. By credibly serving all the aforementioned, Oman became a valuable back channel for warring parties (Baabood 2017, 120). In 2018, Qaboos told the United Nations General Assembly (UNGA) that military action in Yemen would perpetuate power struggles and societal disintegration (Byman 2018, 142). Oman emphasised 'political settlement through dialogue is the only way to achieve peace' (Cafiero and Ulrichsen 2018). Oman conveyed that it sees Yemen's stability as a strategic interest at the UN by stating, 'given our geographic proximity and deep historical, social and cultural ties with Yemen, we emphasise Oman will provide our brother people of Yemen [...]' (UNGA 2019). Oman's diplomatic approach served Qaboos' interest to preserve Oman's soft power in Yemen, and to balance Yemen-GCC relations without sacrificing Oman-Iran relations or Oman-GCC relations.

These non-conformist policies are not without risk. Oman's non-intervention was perceived as a political act by Riyadh and Abu Dhabi. They view Houthi rebels as Iranian proxies and termed Qaboos' policies as 'negative neutrality'. In response, Qaboos attempted to persuade his GCC partners that his 'bridge' role promoted 'positive' contributions that were 'good for all.' Playing 'the Islamic card,' he argued that these roles were 'natural' for Oman given its constitution and its Ibadi heritage. As might be expected, a senior member of Oman's Shura Council chimed in: '[he] couldn't have participated in this coalition. It's in our constitution. We don't send troops or artillery anywhere, unless requested by the United Nations' (Cafiero and Karasik, 2017). The Omani regime believed that Saudi and Emirati activities were destabilizing in Yemen, and allowed 'several terrorist organizations to use Yemen as a base ... [which] poses direct threats', and ran counter to Muscat's interests (UNGA 2015). Muscat's history of internal religious, ideological, and political grievance, and its fundamental distrust of the Saudis, drove its independent policies. In addition, Muscat's suspicions were further heightened by Emirati interventionist meddling in Mahra, Musandam, Sohar, and Zanzibar – traditional areas of Omani influence (Ardemagni 2019; Mtumwa 2018).

In the case of the Qatar Boycott of 2017–2021, Qaboos judged the effort to be counter to Omani interests. Oman adopted the symbols of impartiality by maintaining full relations with all parties and publicly offering to support Kuwait-led diplomatic talks (Baabood 2017, 30). Oman accrued strategic rewards through cooperation with Iran and proximity to the Qatar-Iran-Turkish alignment. Secondly, Riyadh and Abu Dhabi's actions set a precedent for arbitrary aggression against another Arab state, which fuelled views about a need to protect Oman's sovereignty (Kinninmont 2019). Third, given Oman's close relations with the Al Thani in Qatar, Oman backed Doha and its right to pursue policy independent from Riyadh and Abu Dhabi. Next, Oman saw concrete economic advantages in the situation. Muscat opted to give Qatar access to its ports for trans-shipment of food and supplies, it opened up its sea lanes for the export of Qatari LNG, and opened its airspace, allowing Qatar Airways a lifeline – thus bypassing Emirati territory (Economist 2017; Dudley 2017). In return, Oman enhanced its energy, trade, and investment situation by attracting new deals, and it secured more defence cooperation. Finally, Oman's commercial cooperation with Qatar and Iran also reflected a political strategy that emphasizes Muscat's maritime independence. The Duqm port facility, located at a strategic maritime intersection on the Indian Ocean, is designed to attract new cooperating partners to its port. Oman's history imparted beliefs about interconnections between autonomy, regime security, commerce, and geography. This neutral port business model provides opportunities to cooperate with 'user' states like China, India, Japan, South Korea, the US, and UK – thereby potentially enhancing Oman's utility to more powerful states.

Clearly, the Omanis understood that non-cooperation with the blockade offered greater potential benefit than participation. Oman also refuses to participate in personalised political disputes. Oman would likely have equally appreciated the absurdity of Abu Dhabi blockading Qatar and yet buying Qatar/Iranian natural gas through the Dolphin pipeline to power its electrical generators. Plus, after a US policy wobble due to President Donald Trump's idiosyncratic leadership, US pressure to end the dispute soon ramped up as splitting the US-backed Sunni alliance that keeps Iranian aggression at bay was not in the interest of any state involved. For these reasons, the blockade was a failure before it even began (Fahim and DeYoung 2017; Calamur 2016). Furthermore, in Qaboos' defence of his unaligned position, he was able to argue that by cooperating with all GCC states, he indirectly supported the collective Gulf security by not participating in divisive policy toward Qatar. Oman pursued its strategic parochial interests while hiding behind the fig-leaf of 'recogniz[ing] the [GCC's] importance for regional security and economic cooperation' (Baaboud 2017, 30). Oman's policy was neither neutral or even non-interventionist – Muscat sided with Qatar and intervened on behalf of Qatar for its own strategic interests.

Ibadi Islam and Political Pragmatism

The political structure of the Arab Gulf states is authoritarian. They do not reflect (and likely never will reflect) post-French Revolution notions of a national state (Barrett 2016, xxiv–xxvii). The effect of this condition is that the 'regime' or dynasty is the core unit of analysis in an assessment of Gulf states' threat perceptions and national interest (Darwish and Kaarbo 2019, 5). Further, modern national states traditionally create their identity around the concept of nationalism. 'Imagined' or not, it is a potent force that has provided the rationale for unity and justified state coercion to enforce it since the French Revolution (Anderson 1983). Gulf rulers claim Islamic legitimacy but sit atop a dynastic state maintained through tribal patronage. In the Arab Gulf, state-based nationalism remains superficial despite ongoing attempts to artificially manufacture it with infusions of oil revenue through an ancient tribal patronage system. Qaboos embraced the tribal system in Oman as a foundational pillar of stability through which the government flowed jobs, affordable housing, modern healthcare, and educational opportunites. Any serious attempt to transition away from the tribal patronage system, particularly with the post-hydrocarbon world on the horizon, will undoubtedly create challenges to political, economic, and social stability that will be unacceptable to the Al Bu Said regime.

Western-educated, Qaboos understood these linked challenges. He utilised Oman's unique Ibadi heritage to articulate an idealised ideological justification to govern Omani society, but also for domestic and foreign policy that allowed his regime to justify policies based on self-preservation. To avoid conflict, Qaboos' definition of an Ibadi state emphasised consultation, negotiation, tolerance, and avoidance of conflict within an Islamic context. In regional and foreign policy, the Ibadi heritage provided the option of saying that Oman is different from the other regional states and above petty Sunni versus Shi'a arguments. Yet, this religious ideology has frequently been used to justify Oman's refusal to engage in conflicts and to maintain relations with Iran and others. While 'State Ibadi Islam' as conceived by Qaboos represents the politization of a 'manufactured ideology' designed to support Al Bu Said's rule, it is also an ingenious adaptation of Oman's distinct cultural heritage that supports the state's ability to deal with foreign and domestic threats to stability and security.

From 1991 to 2020, Qaboos' policies were coherently structured to safeguard a stability rarely experienced for centuries prior. From the perspective of institutions, history, culture, democracy, and general conceptions of mature anarchy, the Western state milieu is therefore simply not applicable. It cannot accommodate the conditions that correspond to the regional dynamics, historical experiences, governance models, and statehood found in the Arabian Gulf. Oman's present can only be understood within the context of its past – a past that echoes in the present. More importantly, those same echoes will no doubt shape the future as well. Oman is too important to the Gulf security system to ignore, and by appreciating the relevance of its historical and socio-cultural context, scholars and foreign policy practitioners can capture glimpses of the future.

Partisan Non-Intervention in Content

Given the fractured historical context of Oman, the reality of the post-1945 Gulf required a new political structure if Al Bu Said's Oman was going to survive. The Sultanate had no credibility in the area controlled by the Imamate or in Sunni tribal Dhofar. The British were no longer capable of unilaterally defending the Al Bu Said, and new radical Arab nationalist forces offered new ideologies that threatened all traditionalist regimes. Oman's contemporary domestic and foreign policies constituted the informed response to these conditions by a strictly authoritarian leader, Qaboos, who had the ability to design state policy himself. He understood the need to prevent any actor (internal or external) from leveraging Oman's fractured political, economic, and socio-cultural environment. Contemporary Oman simply did not exist prior to 1970 and, despite independence, statehood was in fact not cemented until the 1980s. Qaboos' success in developing and implementing an effective security strategy is the reason why successors are following his policies today.

Fractured Geography and Socio-Cultural Realities

Contemporary Oman is an Arab and an Indian Ocean state composed of conflicting social and cultural traditions complicated by layered tribal conflicts. During the first century CE, Hinawi tribes, claiming Ghatani or pure Arab origins, migrated from Yemen and found themselves in conflict with the Persians and another Arab tribal group, the Ghafiri, or so-called Adnani, of mixed Arab origin (Phillips 1962, 4–7). With the advent of Islam, Hinawi tribes eventually adopted the Ibadi form of Kharijite Islam, viewing it as 'an ancient community rooted in Quranic revelation' that rejected both Sunni orthodoxy or Shi'a sectarianism (Wilkinson 2009, 12). The Ghafiri tribes were largely Sunni, inhabiting the coastal areas. During the seventeenth and eighteenth centuries, the Omani Yaaruba Dynasty (1624–1743) expanded into a vacuum created by the collapse of the Portuguese empire (Wilkinson, 2009, 12). With a powerful navy, the Yaaruba dominated the Arabian and African coasts. In the 1730s, Ghafiiri and Hinawi feuding brought collapse and the re-emergence of the Persians under Nadir Shah (who ruled between 1736–1747), and the emergence of the First Saudi State (1744–1818) fractured Omani power. Then in 1748, a new dynasty emerged, the Al Bu Said, led by Ahmad bin Said bin Mohammed Al Bu Said. Allied with the Ghafiri tribes of the coast, he expelled the Persians, eliminated the Hinawi Yaaruba Imamate entirely and then demanded that the Ibadi *ulema* recognize him as the Al Bu Said.

After the Seven Years' War (1756–1763), involving most European great powers, the British became the dominant power on the Omani littoral and a synergy of interests developed between the Sultanate and British East India Company-ruled India. This confluence of interests centered on threats posed by the rise of the First Saudi State (1744–1818) and its various maritime allies in the region, particularly the Qasimi tribes of Ras al-Khaymah and Sharjah (Risso 1986, 179–180). By 1798, to enhance their control, the British had dictated a treaty with Muscat entrenching themselves in Sultanate affairs (Phillips 1962, 70–72). The Sultan in Muscat had little choice but to acquiesce. British India's control steadily increased. In 1856, the British intervened in a succession crisis with the Canning Award dividing Oman from its African holdings, impoverishing the former (Al-Maamiry 1979, 63–68). Concerned only with the coast, the British failed to understand the implications of their policies on the interior (Badger 1874, 3). Due to British intervention, Ibadi *ulema* (religious authorities), who represented the population of the interior, now viewed the Al Bu Said rulers to be 'little better' than non-believers (Kelly 1980, 110). Despising the British and their Al Bu Said allies, Ghafiri and Hinawi tribes united and declared Sultan Faisal (who ruled between 1888–1913) deposed. Their intent was to establish an 'ideal of the true imamate' (Scholz 1976, 89; Peterson 1978, 30). A century of Al Bu Said political subservience to the British played into the hands of the Ibadi revivalists (Wilkinson 2009, 249–251). The British agent admitted, 'permitting them [*the Sultans*] to misrule without protest has done more to alienate the interior' (Wilkinson 2009, 251).

In 1913, a massive tribal revolt proved to be an eye-opener. Only British intervention saved the Sultanate. The British Resident wrote that the 'government is so bad that to continue to support it in its existing condition is nothing short of immoral'. In July 1920, the British negotiated the Treaty of Sib between the Sultanate and the Imamate whereby the coastal Sultanate was recognised as sovereign, but pledged non-interference in the affairs of the Imamate (PRO, FO 371/114578: 15–16). The jurisdictional ambiguity between Sultanate and Imamate may have served immediate British interests, but it would create future problems. In 1932, Sultan Said (who ruled between 1932–1970) succeeded his father and attempted to consolidate Muscat's authority by reconciling the interior Ibadis with the coastal Sultanate through subsidies to interior tribes, which undermined the Imam's influence (Bierschenk 1989, 123). Stability would prove temporary.

In the 1930s, the discovery of oil and Saudi claims on the Omani and Trucial State interiors upset regional stability. In 1949, Saudi Arabia with ARAMCO's support occupied the disputed Buraimi Oasis. The Foreign Office worried that the extension of Saudi territorial ambitions to central Oman had given rise to 'religious extremists' in the Imamate (PRO, FO371-104294, EA1081/519/G). In 1952, when Said united the Omani tribes to eject the Saudis, the US State Department pressured Britain to pursue talks in Geneva and force Said to stand down (FCO8/62 1967). At this point, the Foreign Office warned Whitehall that Britain 'could not be certain of succeeding in a court of international law' (PRO, FO371/104294, EA1081/518). For Said, the consequence was that the

Imamate launched the 1955 and 1957 rebellions to overthrow him (Townsend 1977, 62). Both Saudi Arabia and Nasserist Egypt backed the tribal opponents of the Al Bu Said and supported Ghalib bin 'Ali Al-Hinai (1912–2009), the last Ibadi Imam. The latter declared an independent imamate and applied for Arab League membership (PRO, FO371/114613, EA1081/603). In 1955, the British forcibly removed the Saudis from Buraimi and began acting against the Imamate (PRO, FO371/114578, EA1015/21). Largely suppressed by 1959, unrest continued into the 1960s. Nevertheless, the situation destroyed Said's credibility (Holden 1966, 107). The entire episode provides another example that supports contemporary Oman's obsession with protecting their prerogatives for independent decision-making.

It was at this point that a rebellion broke out in Dhofar. A badly administered personal holding of the Sultan, Dhofar had stronger ethnic and tribal ties to Yemen than Muscat. Said had failed to address economic grievances that interacted with ideology and religion (Peterson 1978, 13). Oman was so divided it was officially called 'Muscat and Oman ... and Dhofar' (Beasant 2013, 61; Hiro 2003). In 1965, multiple opposition groups formed the Dhofar Liberation Front (DLF), and declared that 'the hireling regime under its ruler, Said bin Taymour, will be destroyed'. In 1967, the DLF transformed into the 'Front for the Liberation of the Occupied Arabian Gulf', replete with leftist slogans and policies (Al-Maamiry 1979, 115, 218–225). For years, members of the Al Bu Said had called for the Sultan's removal (Peterson 2013, 233–234). On July 23, 1970, with British support, Qaboos and his allies mounted a coup and forced Said to abdicate (Rigsbee and Allen 2014, 238–241). By then, Oman had a ruler with new ideas about the future.

Qaboos, Independence, and the Way Forward

In 1970, Qaboos' accession to the throne created a bridge to a new synthesis that more accurately reflected the reality of the Oman, both old and new. Born in Salalah to the daughter of a Dhofari paramount sheikh and Sultan Said, Qaboos physically embodied the most diverse components of state. He was also the beneficiary of a formal education in Britain and a graduate of Sandhurst Military Academy. After service with the British Army and additional studies in government, Qaboos returned to Oman in 1966. Sultan Said correctly surmised that the British were grooming his successor and put Qaboos under virtual house arrest. Qaboos' perspective was not that of a cloistered heir. From 1970 to 1972, Omani and British forces, joined by Jordanian and Iranian units, curbed the revolt (Peterson 2013, 325–333). Horrified by Iranian forces on the Arabian Peninsula, Riyadh increased financial support (Gause 1990, 128). Qaboos clearly grasped the advantages of triangulation and multiple sources of security cooperation.

Qaboos understood that Oman's ethnic, sectarian, and tribal divisions required reform which could be supported by strong security services that could neutralize threats to the authority of the Sultan. Oman was also the beneficiary of the dramatic oil price increase resulting from the 1973 Arab oil embargo. The new Sultan also comprehended the relationship between Oman's internal stability, economic well-being, and the role a carefully orchestrated non-interventionist foreign policy played in both. By coupling a subset of carefully selected Ibadi principles with its multicultural Indian Ocean maritime openness and Gulf Arab heritage, Oman charted an independent path within the regional and international context that suited its partisan requirements. The Sultan rejected with equanimity Kharijite, Sunni, and Shi'a doctrine as a justification for sectarian or political strife. He linked Salalah and the cities and towns of the old Imamate to Muscat with economic and transportation infrastructure improvements. The Sultan focused on the role of tribes in society as 'an essential element to promote national unity and political legitimacy' (Dekmajian 2001, 308). Qaboos shrewdly gave each group a stake in his integrated state. This inclusiveness, the bedrock of post-independence internal stability, mirrors Oman's external 'friend to all' approach, underscoring its underlying philosophy on non-aligned stances.

This process did not occur overnight. The Dhofar issue only fully disappeared with the 1986 South Yemen Civil War and the 1991 collapse of the Soviet Union. The problems associated with neo-Ibadi fundamentalism flared from time to time in the interior, which have been followed by various Sunni Islamic fundamentalist threats. In this case, the Sultanate followed a zero-tolerance policy for dissent or political Islamic movements. Yet, Qaboos created the *Majlis al-Istishari li al-Dawla* (State Consultative Council, or SCC) in 1981 to allow 'a larger measure of participation for the citizens in the economic and social plans'. Although closely controlled, the SCC won the right to review social and economic legislation prior to the Sultan's approval. In 1991, the *Majlis al-Shura* (Consultative Council, or CC) replaced the SCC. Apportioned based on population with a high degree of 'urban' tribal representation, some believed that it would eventually lead to direct elections (Rigsbee and Allen 2014, 48–56). But that was never going to happen. Sultan Qaboos took the lessons of Oman's history of instability, strife, and foreign intervention, and tailored a set of policies – both foreign and domestic – that suppressed centrifugal forces that had always plagued Omani rulers, whether imams or sultans. Under Qaboos, Omani policy eschewed intervention of any kind in the internal affairs of other states and focused on an independent path in the region governed by pragmatic self-interest. This was not neutrality – it was recognition of the limited ability of Oman's small state to affect external events, and the challenges of maintaining its own territorial integrity. In addition, survival of the state ultimately depended on the backing of a capable superpower willing to support the Al Bu Said – the US.

The Al Bu Said and the Future

Upon Sultan Qaboos' death in January 2020, his first cousin, Haitham bin Tariq bin Taymur Al Bu Said, inherited Oman's contradictions and potential for instability. He accepted a modern state whose foreign policy linked Oman's strategic security posture to the US' without surrendering its range of partnerships across regional political divides, making Oman a useful option for many seeking to have difficult dialogues. Sultan Haitham also retained the tight-lipped opacity and discretion that Qaboos' regime was famous for, and his authoritarian control exercised through highly efficient internal security services. Haitham's lack of hands-on experience in the military or the security services did not appear to detract from his stature. The new Sultan promised to 'preserve' what Qaboos had created and 'build on it' (Aman 2020). However, it is difficult to imagine that he wields anything close to the absolute authority of his predecessor (Fisher 2013). He is thus more collegial and needs consensus-based arrangements that involve buy-in from key officials and tribal leaders.

Under Sultan Haitham, Omani foreign policy efforts focus on economic growth and deeper levels of rapprochement between Muscat, Riyadh, and Abu Dhabi after ties were strained by issues like Qatar and Yemen, the 2011 intervention in Bahrain, rejecting the 2013 Gulf Union proposal as well as perceptions that Muscat went 'behind their backs' in 2015 by helping negotiate the 2015 nuclear deal. On one hand, Sultan Haitham's pursuit of better relations with Riyadh and the UAE are designed to help Muscat contribute to peace in Yemen, which Oman seeks for its own security. On the other hand, Oman stands to benefit from reduced tensions with Saudi Arabia and the UAE on various other fronts such as Oman's border regions, but also from economic development opportunities. For example, there is a new desert highway linking Ibri in Oman and al-Ahsa in Saudi Arabia that bypasses UAE territory and the Straits of Hormuz, creating new prospects for developing port facilities at Duqm on the Indian Ocean (Cafiero 2021).

The new regime has yet to face a crisis on the level of the Arab Spring. Qaboos had the stature to blame ministers and replace them. Assuming a more consensus-driven power structure, it is unclear if Sultan Haitham has that level of unilateral power. In addition, the Omani government will continue to face continued economic pressure, perhaps even more critical than that faced by Qaboos. With a growing percentage of the population under 30 years of age, and an estimated 30 per cent of that group unemployed, the "social pressure" and potential for political unrest remains. Declining oil reserves present an unprecedented challenge. Despite this, there are signs that the immediate economic situation has improved. The deficit fell from 16.1 per cent of GDP in 2020 to 3.4 per cent in 2021. Although half of this decline was due in large part to the increased price of oil, an improvement in non-oil related revenue accounted for the remainder, including cautious scaling back of water and electricity subsidies. Sultan Haitham is credited for maintaining the momentum for economic reform, but he is no doubt mindful that reforms that look good to an economist on paper sometimes have negative effects on stability (Dudley 2021).

Sultan Haitham is following the independent policies that served his predecessor well. In addition to its geographical position, Oman's value also resides in its ability to facilitate dialogue between conflicting entities in the region. As one commentator put it, 'Oman should hold fast to its reputation as a neutral anchor of peace' (Keeler 2020). Sultan Haitham's educational background and ministerial position suggests that he understands that the unity and cohesion Sultan Qaboos' rule brought obscured the historical norm of internal conflict and division. References to Sultan Qaboos as 'the Father of Oman' underscores this stark dichotomy between what came before Qaboos and what came after 1970 (Aman 2020). Sultan Haitham is not Qaboos, nor does he need to be. He merely needs to consolidate his rule and guarantee that the next succession is orderly. During his first year of rule, Sultan Haitham's amendment of the Basic Law (succession) enabled him to designate his oldest son, Dhi Yasan bin Haitham (b. 1990) as Crown Prince. Haitham understands the need for continuity and stability in Omani successions, but the real issue has now become – will the next succession be orderly?

Those hoping for the Council of Oman to acquire the 'power to translate these new articles into law and enforce them with legal guarantees that support and protect public liberties, full political participation for citizens, and an active and free society' will likely be frustrated (al-Zobadi 2021). For Sultan Haitham, the perils of the traditional 'open' Omani succession process outweighed the risks of formalised primogeniture. The potential for instability never disappears – it mutates. Groups shift allegiances, ideologies change, outside support fluctuates, but the underlying sources of instability remain (Ismaik 2022).

For over 250 years, Oman experienced limited periods of stability and extended periods of turmoil and conflict. This left the current regime highly attuned to the role freedom of action and economic self-sufficiency plays in preserving the regime through maintaining internal stability, and external independence of action. It is not an ideological commitment to 'neutrality' as an ideal, but rather a result of hard lessons learned about survival in an unforgiving geopolitical environment. The Omani regime has used every tool at its disposal: the politization of its unique Ibadi religious tradition, a non-interventionist foreign policy, its commitment to diplomacy through openness, and its pragmatic reliance on security ties with the West – the ultimate guarantor of regime and state survival. Derived from lessons from a difficult past, Muscat's pragmatic application of partisan non-intervention were key to Qaboos' success and will likely shape Omani policies in the future.

References

Abuozzohour, Yasmina. 2020. "As Oman enters a new era". *Brookings.* January 15. https://www.brookings.edu/articles/as-oman-enters-a-new-era-economic-and-political-challenges-persist/

Al-Bu'Saidi, Badr bin Hamad. 2005. "Small States' Diplomacy in the Age of Globalization: An Omani Perspective". In *Analyzing Middle East Foreign Policy and The Relationship with Europe*. 258–259. New York: Routledge.

Al-Jaber, Khalid, and Giorgio Cafiero. 2017. "The GCC'S Worst Summit". https://bit.ly/2GRU3mr

Al-Jaber, Khalid. 2020. "Kuwait, Balancer in the Gulf". Gulf International Forum. https://gulfif.org/kuwait-balancer-in-the-gulf

Al-Khalili, Majid. 2009. Oman's Foreign Policy. Westport, Conn.: Praeger Security International.

Al-Khalili, Majid. 2009. *Oman's Foreign Policy: Foundation and Practice.* Westport, Connecticut: Praeger Security International.

Al-Maamiry, Ahmed Hamud. 1979. *Oman and East Africa*. New Delhi: Lancers Books.

Al-Makahleh, Shehab. 2013. "Duqm Port an Alternative for Exporting Gulf Oil". *Gulf News*, 2013. http://gulfnews.com/news/uae/general/duqm-port-an-alternative-forexporting-gulf-oil-1.1211503

Al-Rawas's, Isam. 2000. *Oman in Early Islamic History*. London: Ithaca Press.

Al-Talei, Rafiah. 2021. "What Oman's Constitutional Change Means for Omanis," *Carnegie Endowment for International Peace*. January 14. https://carnegieendowment.org/2021/01/14/what-oman-s-constitutional-change-means-for-omanis-pub-83634

Al-Zobaidi, Haitham. 2021. "Oman's balanced perspective on regulating succession". *The Arab Weekly*. January 19. https://thearabweekly.com/omans-balanced-perspective-regulating-succession

Agwani, M.S. 1981. "The Arab World and Non-Alignment". *International Studies.* 20 (1–2): 371–377. doi:10.1177/002088178102000127.

Allen, Calvin H, and W. Lynn Rigsbee. 2000. *Oman Under Qaboos: From Coup to Constitution, 1970–1996*. London: Frank Cass.

Aman, Martine Denis (host). 2020. Comments of Dr. Houchang Hassan-Yari, Professor of International Relations and Security at Sultan Qaboos University in "What legacy does Sultan Qaboos leave for Oman?". *Inside Story – Al Jazeera* (video). January 11. https://www.aljazeera.com/program/inside-story/2020/1/11/what-legacy-does-sultan-qaboos-leave-for-oman

Aman, Martine Denis (host). 2020. "What legacy does Sultan Qaboos leave for Oman?". *Inside Story – Al Jazeera* (video). January 11. https://www.aljazeera.com/program/inside-story/2020/1/11/what-legacy-does-sultan-qaboos-leave-for-oman

Anderson, Benedict. 1983. *Imagined Communities: Reflections on the Origins and Spread of Nationalism.* New York: Verso Press.

Ardemagni, Eleonora. 2019. "Strategic Borderlands: The UAE-Oman Rivalry Benefits Tehran". Italian Institute for International Political Studies. https://www.ispionline.it/en/pubblicazione/strategic-borderlands-uae-oman-rivalrybenefits-tehran-23347

Baabood, Abdulla. 2017a. "Oman's Independent Foreign Policy". In *The Small Gulf States: Foreign and Security Policies Before and After the Arab Spring*. 107–122. London: Routledge.

Baabood, Abdullah. 2017b. "Oman and the Gulf Diplomatic Crisis". *Oxford Gulf and Arabian Peninsula Forum (Oxgaps).* Autumn: 30–31.

Badr Bin Hamd Al Bu Said. 2003. "Small States' Diplomacy in the Age of Globalization: An Omani Perspective". *Review of International Affairs*. 3, no. 2. https://doi.org/10.1080/1475355032000240748.

Bakir, Ali. 2019. "The Evolution of Turkey—Qatar Relations Amid a Growing Gulf Divide". In *Divided Gulf: The Anatomy of a Crisis*. 197–215. Palgrave Macmillan.

Barrett, Roby C. 2011a. *Oman: The Present in the Context of a Fractured Past*. Hurlburt Field, Fla.: JSOU Press.

Barrett, Roby C. 2011b. *Yemen: A Different Political Paradigm in Context*. MacDill Air Force Base, Fla.: JSOU Press.

Barrett, Roby C. 2016. *The Gulf and the Struggle for Hegemony*. Washington, D.C.: The Middle East Institute and Friesens Corporation.

Beasant, John. 2013. *Oman: The True-Life Drama and Intrigue of An Arab State*. 2nd ed. Edinburgh: Mainstream Publishers.

Bin Huwaidin, Mohamed. 2002. *China's Relations with Arabia and the Gulf, 1949–1999*. London: Routledge.

Bin-Abood, Saif Mohammad Obaid. 1992. "Britain's Withdrawal from the Gulf: With Particular Reference to the Emirates". PhD Dissertation, Durham University.

Boussois, Sébastien. 2019. "Iran and Qatar: A Forced Rapprochement". In *Divided Gulf: The Anatomy of a Crisis*. 217–232. London: Palgrave Macmillan.

Burrows, B. 1990. *Footnotes in the Sand: The Gulf in Transition, 1953–1958*. Norwich: Michael Russell Publishing.

Byman, Daniel. 2018. "Yemen's Disastrous War". *Survival*. 60 (5): 141–158. doi:10.1080/00396338.2018.1518376.

Cafiero, Giorgio. 2021. "What is driving Oman and Saudi Arabia closer?" *Responsible Statecraft*. July 29. https://responsiblestatecraft.org/2021/07/29/what-is-driving-saudi-arabia-and-oman-closer/

Cafiero, Giorgio, and Kristian Coates Ulrichsen. 2018. "Oman's Pragmatic Yemen Foreign Policy: Poised for Promoting Peace?". *Inside Arabia*. https://insidearabia.com/omanpragmatic-yemen-foreign-policy-peace/

Cafiero, Giorgio, and Theodore Karasik. 2016. "Can Oman's Stability Outlive Sultan Qaboos?". Washington, DC: Middle East Institute. https://www.mei.edu/publications/can-omans-stability-outlive-sultan-qaboos

Cafiero, Giorgio. 2015. "Oman Breaks from GCC on Yemen Conflict". *Al Monitor*. http://www.al-monitor.com/pulse/originals/2015/05/oman-response-yemenconflict

Cafiero, Giorgio, and Theodore Karasik. 2017. "Kuwait, Oman, And the Qatar Crisis". Washington, D.C.: Middle East Institute.

Cafiero, Giorgio, and Theodore Karasik. 2017. "Yemen War and Qatar Crisis Challenge Oman's Neutrality". Washington, D.C: Middle East Institute. https://www.mei.edu/publications/yemen-war-and-qatar-crisis-challenge-omans-neutrality

Calamur, Krishnadev. 2017. "Tillerson Calls Qatar's Position in Dispute with Arab States 'Very Reasonable'". 11 July. *The Atlantic*. https://www.theatlantic.com/news/archive/2017/07/qatar-tillerson/533259/

Casey, Michael S. 2007. *The History of Kuwait*. London: Greenwood Press.

Chatham House. 2015. "Yemen: Key Players and Prospects for Peace". 17–18 November: Middle East and North Africa Programme Workshop Summary. https://www.chathamhouse.org/sites/files/chathamhouse/events/2015-11-07-yemenkey-players-prospects-peace-meeting-summary_4.pdf

Cüneyt Mustafa, Özşahin. 2020. "Qatar–Turkey Rapprochement: Challenging the Regional Status Quo in the Gulf Security Sub-Complex". In *The 2017 Gulf Crisis: An Interdisciplinary Approach*, 35–49. Springer.

Darwich, May, and Juliet Kaarbo. 2019. "IR in the Middle East: Foreign Policy Analysis in Theoretical Approaches". *International Relations*, 1–21.

DeVore, Marc. R. 2011. "The United Kingdom's Last Hot War of the Cold War: Oman, 1963–75". *Cold War History*. 1-32. doi:10.1080/14682745.2010.498823.

Dudley, Dominic. 2017. "A Winner Emerges from the Qatar Crisis: Oman's National Airline". *Forbes*. https://www.forbes.com/sites/dominicdudley/2017/06/08/omanair-takes-advantage-of-qatar-crisis/#46f2a6ce25b4

Dekmejian, R.l Hrair. 2001."Forging Institutions in the Gulf Arab States," *Iran, Iraq and the Gulf Arab States*, edited by Joseph A Kechichian. New York: Palgrave.

Dudley, Dominic. 2021. "Fitch Revises Oman's Outlook Up To Stable, Amid Improving State Finances," *Forbes.* December 20. https://www.forbes.com/sites/dominicdudley/2021/12/20/fitch-revises-omans-outlook-up-to-stable-amid-improving-state-finances/?sh=6424f8094cb0

Economist. 2017. "Oman Opens Up Shipping Routes to Qatar". *Country.Eiu. Com*. http://country.eiu.com/article.aspx?articleid=835568667&Country=Qatar&topic=Economy&subtopic=Fore_7

Euler Hermes, Euler. 2017. "Oman Country Economy: Risk Analyses by EH Economic Research". *Eulerhermes.Com*. http://www.eulerhermes.com/economicresearch/country-reports/Pages/Oman.aspx

Ezzat, Noha. 2019. "Oman: Institutional Genealogy of an Exceptional Foreign Policy". In *GCC: Evaluation, Lessons Learned and Future Prospects*. https://www.dur.ac.uk/imeis/events/?eventno=42758

Fahim, Kareem, and Karen DeYoung. 2017. "Four Arab Nations Sever Diplomatic Ties with Qatar, Exposing Rift in Region". *The Washington Post*. https://www.washingtonpost.com/world/four-arab-nations-sever-diplomatic-ties-with-qatar-exposing-rift-in-region/2017/06/05/15ad2284-49b4-11e7-9669-250d0b15f83b_story.html

Fahy, Michael. 2016. "China's Investment in $10.7Bn City in Oman to Provide Building". *The National*, 2016. https://www.thenational.ae/business/property/china-sinvestment-in-10-7bn-city-in-oman-to-provide-building-boost-1.169865

Fanack News. 2018. "Neutral Oman Braces for Challenges Ahead Amid Sultan's Ailing Health". https://fanack.com/politics/features-insights/neutral-oman-braces-challenges-amid-sultans-ailing-health~97991/

FCO 8/1710. 1971. "Arabic Tropical Programs: Friday, 2.7.71".

FCO 08/62. 1967. "Foreign Commonwealth Office: Confidential: Qateri Interest in The Buraimi Question: 6 February 1967".

FCO 08/1676. 1971. "Confidential: Record of a Meeting with Tariq: 3 May 1971".

FCO 8/5814. 1985 Jan 01 - 1985 Dec 31. "Gulf Heads of Mission Conference, Bahrain".

FCO 8/574. 1967–1968. "Muscat and Oman: Political Affairs (Internal), Sultan of Muscat".

Fisher, Amanda. 2015. "The case of the sealed envelope: Oman's path to succession," *Middleeasteye.net*. January 13. http://www.middleeasteye.net/in-depth/features/case-sealed-envelope-oman-s-path-succession-567113540

Funsch, Linda Pappas. 2015. *Oman Reborn: Balancing Tradition and Modernization*. New York: Palgrave Macmillan.

Gorvett, Jonathan. 2018. "Oman Plans Pipeline to Iran as US Sanctions Loom". *Asia Times*, 2018. http://www.atimes.com/article/oman-plans-pipeline-to-iran-as-us-sanctionsloom/

Gunther, Michael. 2020. "Sultan Qaboos of Oman's Policy of Strategic Neutrality". Defence-in-Depth: Defence Studies Department, King's College London. https://defenceindepth.co/2020/02/05/sultan-qaboos-of-omans-policy-of-strategicneutrality/

Hamidaddin, Abdullah. 2013. "Oman and the GCC: A Policy Of 'Don't Stand So Close to Me?'". *Al Arabiya*, 2013. http://english.alarabiya.net/en/views/news/middleeast/2013/12/08/Oman-and-the-GCC-A-policy-of-don-t-stand-so-close-to-me-.html

Harb, Imad. 2018. "Determinants of Oman's Strategic Position on the Gulf Crisis". Arab Centre Washington D.C. http://arabcenterdc.org/policy_analyses/determinants-ofomans-strategic-position-on-the-gulf-crisis/

Holden, David. 1966. *Farewell to Arabia*. London: Faber and Faber.

Gause III, F. Gregory. 1990. *Saudi-Yemen Relations: Domestic Structures and Foreign Influence.* New York: Columbia University Press.

Hiro, Dilip. 2003. *The Essential Middle East: A Comprehensive Guide.* New York: Carroll & Graf Publishers.

Ibn Razik, Salih. 1872. *History of the Imams and Seyyids of 'Oman from A.D. 661 to 1856*, translated by George Percy Badger. London: The Hakluyt Society.

Iran News. 2020. "Tehran Eyes Expanding Economic Ties with Muscat". *Iran News*. https://irannewsdaily.com/2020/07/tehran-eyes-expanding-economic-ties-with-muscat/

Ismaik, Hasan. 2022. "Why Oman didn't join the Abraham Accords". The Jerusalem Post. February 1. https://www.jpost.com/opinion/article-695221

Jones, Jeremy, and Nicholas Peter Ridout. 2012. *Oman, Culture and Diplomacy.* Edinburgh: Edinburgh University Press.

Karasik, Theodore, and Stephen Blank. 2017. "Russia in The Middle East". Jamestown Foundation. https://jamestown.org/press-releases/jamestown-launches-russia-middleeast-project/

Kéchichian, Joseph A. 1985. "The Gulf Cooperation Council: Search for Security". *Third World Quarterly.* 7 (4): 853–881.

Kéchichian, Joseph A. 1995. *Oman And the World: The Emergence of an Independent Foreign Policy.* Santa Monica, CA: Rand.

Kechichian, Joseph A. 2016. *From Alliance to Union: Challenges Facing Gulf Cooperation Council States.* Sussex Academic Press.

Kelly, J.B. 1980. *Arabia, the Gulf, & the West.* London: George Weidenfield and Nicolson Limited.

Keeler, Louisa. 2020. "Can Oman Survive Its Own Neighborhood After the Death of Sultan Qaboos?" *Foreign Policy Research Institute*. January 21. https://www.fpri.org/article/2020/01/can-oman-survive-its-own-neighborhood-after-the-death-of-sultan-qaboos/

Khatib, Dania Koleilat. 2020. "A Turkish-Saudi Rapprochement Could Promote Stability in The Region". Near East South Asia Centre for Strategic Studies. https://nesacenter. org/a-turkish-saudi-rapprochement-can-promote-stability-in-the-region/

Kinninmont, Jane. 2019. "The Gulf Divided the Impact of the Qatar Crisis". Chatham House Middle East and North Africa Programme.

Kochan, Ran. 1972. "Changing Emphasis in The Non-Aligned Movement". *The World.* 28 (11): 501–508.

Lefebvre, Jeffrey A. 2010. "Oman's Foreign Policy in the Twenty-First Century". *Middle East Policy.* 17 (1): 99–114. doi:10.1111/j.1475-4967.2010.00429.x

Lienhardt, Peter. 2001. "Shaikhdoms of Eastern Arabia". St Antony's Series: Oxford University. Palgrave Macmillan.

Lons, Camille. 2019. "Onshore Balancing: The Threat to Oman's Neutrality". https://www.ecfr.eu/article/commentary_onshore_balancing_the_threat_to_omans_neutrality

Louis, Roger. 2003. "The British Withdrawal from the Gulf, 1967–71". *The Journal of Imperial and Commonwealth History.* 31 (1): 83–108.

National Archives – Public Records Office (PRO). Kew: UK.

Michel, David, and Russell Sticklor. 2012. "Indian Ocean Rising: Maritime Security and Policy Challenges". July. Stimson.

Mtumwa, Haji. 2018. "Tanzania: UAE to Open Consulate in Zanzibar". https://allafrica.com/stories/201812140099.html

Mubasher. 2017. "Oman Borrows $3.6Bn Unsecured Term Loan from China – Oman News Agency". *English.Mubasher.Info.* https://english.mubasher.info/news/3141438/Omanborrows-3-6bn-unsecured-term-loan-from-China-ONA

Mustafa Cüneyt, Özşahin. 2020. "Qatar–Turkey Rapprochement: Challenging the Regional Status Quo in the Gulf Security Sub-Complex". In The 2017 *Gulf Crisis: An Interdisciplinary Approach.* 35–49. Springer.

Neubauer, Sigurd. 2016. "Yemen's Warring Sides Finally Met at Talks, But What's Next?". Washington, D.C.: Arab Gulf States Institute in Washington. http://www.agsiw.org/yemens-warring-sides-finally-met-at-talks-but-whats-next

Neubauer, Sigurd. 2016. "Oman: The Gulf's Go-Between". Issue Paper 1. Washington: The Arab Gulf States Institute.

Peterson, J.E. 1978. *Oman in The Twentieth Century: Political Foundations of An Emerging State*. London: Croom Helm and Barnes Noble.

Peterson, J.E. 2013. *Oman's Insurgencies: The Sultanate's Struggle for Supremacy.* United Kingdom: Saqi.

Peterson, J.E. 1984. "Legitimacy and Political Change in Yemen and Oman". *Orbis.* 27 (4): 971–998.

Phillips, Wendell. 1962. *Oman: A History*. London: William Morrow & Company.

Riggs, Robert J. 2020. "The Qatar–Iran–Turkey Nexus: Shifts in Political Alliances and Economic Diversification in the Gulf Crisis". In *The 2017 Gulf Crisis: An Interdisciplinary Approach*, 181–191. Springer.

Riphenburg, C.J. 1998. *Oman: Political Development in A Changing World*. Westport, CT: Praeger.

Risso, Patricia. 1986. *Oman and Muscat: An Early Modern History*. London: Croom Helm Limited.

Rigsbee II, W. Lynn., Allen, Calvin H. 2014. *Oman Under Qaboos: From Coup to Constitution, 1970–1996*. Taylor & Francis.

Sailer, Matthias, and Stephan Roll. 2017. "Three Scenarios for the Qatar Crisis Regime Change, Resolution or Cold War in the Gulf". German Institute for International and Security Affairs. https://www.swpberlin.org/fileadmin/contents/products/comments/2017C25_sil_rll.pdf

Salisbury, Peter. 2015. "Yemen and the Saudi–Iranian 'Cold War'". Research Paper (February). Middle East and North Africa Programme: Chatham House.

Sayegh, Fayez A. 1964. *The Dynamics of Neutralism in the Arab World: A Symposium*. San Francisco, California: Chandler Pub. Co.

Scholz, Fred. *Entwicklungstendenzen in Beduinentum der Kleinen Staaten am Persischen-Arabischen Golf–Oman als Beispiel*. Vienna: Mitteilungen der Osterreichischen Geographischen Gesellschaft, 1976.

Sheline, Annelle. 2020. "Oman's Smooth Transition Doesn't Mean Its Neighbors Won't Stir Up Trouble". *Foreign Policy*. https://foreignpolicy.com/2020/01/23/omans-smoothtransition-saudi-arabia-uae-mbs-stir-up-trouble/

Sherwood, Leah. 2017a. "Understanding Oman's Foreign Policy". *Oxford Gulf and Arabian Peninsula Studies*. Autumn 2017: 11–13.

Steinberg, Guido. 2020. "Regional Power United Arab Emirates Abu Dhabi is No Longer Saudi Arabia's Junior Partner". Research Paper. 2020/RP 10 (July). The German Institute for International and Security Affairs, SWP. http://doi:10.18449/2020RP10

Tehran Times. 2019. "Oman Trying to Expand Economic Ties with Iran". *Tehran Times*. https://www.tehrantimes.com/news/442748/Oman-trying-to-expand-economicties-with-Iran

Tètreault, Mary Ann. 1991. "Autonomy, Necessity, and the Small State: Ruling Kuwait in the Twentieth Century". *International Organization*. 45 (4): 565–591. doi:10.1017/s002081830003321x.

Toumi, Habib. 2019. "Oman: No Solution in Sight for Qatar Crisis". *Gulf News*. https://gulfnews.com/world/gulf/oman/oman-no-solution-in-sight-for-qatar-crisis-1.62767417

Townsend, John. 1977. *Oman*. London: C. Helm.

Wilkinson, John C. 2009. *The Imamate Tradition of Oman*. Cambridge: Cambridge University Press.

Umar, Baba. 2016. "Yemen's War Wounded Find Comfort In 'Brotherly' Oman". *Senegal News Wire*. https://senegalnewswire.com/author/baba-umar/

United Nations General Assembly (UNGA). 2019. "Seventy-Fourth Session 6th Plenary Meeting. 25 September. New York. A/74/PV.6."

United Nations General Assembly (UNGA). 2019. "Yemen: Collective Failure, Collective Responsibility – UN Expert Report. Ohchr.Org.

United Nations General Assembly (UNGA). 2015. "Seventieth Session 28th Plenary Meeting". 3 October. New York. A/70/PV.28."

Vital, D. 1967. *The Inequality of States: A Study of The Small Power in International Relations*. Oxford: Oxford University Press.

Wilkinson, John C. 1987. *The Imamate Tradition of Oman*. London: Cambridge University Press.

Wintour, Patrick. 2020. "This Article Is More Than 2 Months Old Breakthrough in Qatar Dispute After 'Fruitful' Talks to End Conflict". *The Guardian*. https://www.theguardian.com/world/2020/dec/04/breakthrough-in-qatar-dispute-afterfruitful-talks-to-end-conflict

Yadav Philbrick, Stacey. 2017. "Oman is a Mediator in Yemen. Can It Play the Same Role in Qatar?". *Washington Post*. https://www.washingtonpost.com/news/monkey-cage/wp/2017/07/22/oman-is-a-mediator-in-yemen-can-it-play-the-same-role-in-qatar/

Young, Karen. 2019. "The Gulf's Eastward Turn: The Logic of Gulf-China Economic Ties". *Journal Of Arabian Studies*. 9 (2): 236–252. doi:10.1080/21534764.2019.1768655.

Note on Indexing

Our books do not have indexes due to the prohibitive cost of assembling them. If you are reading this book in paperback and want to find a particular word or phrase you can do so by downloading a free PDF version of this book from the E-International Relations website. View the e-book in any standard PDF reader and enter your search terms in the search box. You can then navigate through the search results and find what you are looking for. If you are using apps (or devices) to read our e-books, you should also find word search functionality in those.

You can find all of our books at https://www.e-ir.info/publications/

www.ingramcontent.com/pod-product-compliance
Lightning Source LLC
Chambersburg PA
CBHW071214020426
42333CB00015B/1403